THE TRIAL OF BENAZIR

BY THE SAME AUTHOR:

Non-fiction

A Study of Nehru
Rise of Muslims in Indian Politics
The Struggle within Islam
Hundred Glorious Years

Fiction

Razia: Queen of India
Price of Power

THE TRIAL OF BENAZIR

Rafiq Zakaria

BOMBAY
POPULAR PRAKASHAN

POPULAR PRAKASHAN PRIVATE LIMITED
35-C, Pandit Madan Mohan Malaviya Marg,
Popular Press Bldg., Tardeo, Bombay 400 034.

Typeset in 11/12 pts. Palatino by The Typesetters,
93, Bombay Samachar Marg, Bombay 400 023.
Designed by: P.S. Sathe
Printed in India by Rekha Printers Pvt. Ltd.,
A-102/1, Okhala Industrial Area, Phase II, New Delhi
and Published by Ramdas Bhatkal
for Popular Prakashan Pvt. Ltd.,
35-C, Pandit Madan Mohan Malaviya Marg,
Bombay 400 034.

Some time ago, a friend came to me and barraged me with questions about the status of woman in Islam.

He had many misgivings. I cleared some but to several of his questions, I did not have ready answers. He put more doubts in my mind when he left than I had when he came to me.

I decided to find out the right answers. I went wherever I could, on the highways as well as the bylanes of knowledge. I met the devout as also the sceptic; I talked to the fundamentalist and to the secularist. I fathomed deep to get at the roots; I gathered all that I could.

I don't know how far I have succeeded in my endeavour; but I feel more confident about the answers now than I was when the doubts disturbed my mind.

As my friend left me, he recited to me an ancient prayer:

> *From the cowardice, which makes us*
> > *shrink from the truth;*
> *From the laxness, which makes us*
> > *content with half-truth;*
> *From the arrogance, which makes us*
> > *believe that we know all truth*
> *O my Lord, deliver us.*

To my friend, who prefers to remain anonymous,
I dedicate
this humble effort of mine, in the pursuit of truth.

CONTENTS

Every striver strives
According to his light;
And only Allah knows
Who is, how far, right.

— Quran (17:84)

PREFACE

The emergence of Benazir Bhutto, a 35-year-old, modern, western educated, unveiled, sophisticated, beautiful Muslim woman as Prime Minister of the most powerful Muslim state in the world created quite a stir in November 1988. It was generally believed that a woman could never be allowed by the faithful to assume political power. Certainly not in a Muslim state and most certainly not in Pakistan, the bastion of Muslim orthodoxy. But it happened. And happened despite the heavy doses of the so-called "Islamisation" that the military dictator, General Zia-ul-Haq, gave to the Pakistanis for over eleven years. Zia was backed by the foremost fundamentalist organisation in South Asia, the Jamaat-i-Islami, whose widespread network carried the Zia mission forward to every nook and corner of Pakistan. And yet when the people of Pakistan were called upon to vote, they chose Zia's arch rival and an avowed secularist, Benazir Bhutto as their leader.

The Ulama, (the learned theologians), who had been campaigning against the appointment of a woman as head of an Islamic state since the process of constitution-making began in Pakistan in the early fifties, were most upset at this development. They protested, they called a convention, and they decided to use every device to upset the popular verdict. In the following chapter, the *Introduction*, I have narrated the sequence of events, culminating in Benazir's election as Prime Minister of Pakistan.

The matter has attracted world-wide attention; it has naturally led to the discussion of the larger issue of the status of woman in Islam. The Muslim press has debated it thread bare; there is an increasing interest in the subject

IX

all around. I have, therefore, devised a novel method of finding the truth about Islam's treatment of women. I have put up Benazir Bhutto for trial before an Islamic tribunal, which would decide whether Islam permits her to head the government of an Islamic state. Using the trial as a platform, I have brought forth legendary figures from Islam's past and present to express their views. They represent opinions of all shades of the spectrum. I have drawn largely from the published works of these great men of learning, using their own arguments and points of view. In many cases, the words they use in this trial are their own. Some liberty has, no doubt, been taken in order to knit together the different and variant propositions but by and large, the stand that these scholars have taken in this trial is the same as they had taken in their times on similar issues. Their views reflect the general trend of their contributions to Islamic jurisprudence.

The tribunal, which I have constituted for this purpose, must inspire universal confidence among Muslims the world over. The seven Imams are the finest interpretators of the laws, regulations and practices of Islam. They head either the various Sunni schools of theology or represent the ultimate in Islamic jurisprudence. The law applicable in this case has to be Sunni as both, the petitioners and the respondent, belong to the Sunni sect of Muslims.

While the *Introduction* deals with factual events, the subsequent chapters are set in an imaginary world where the distinction between the living and the dead is obliterated. Men and women from the annals of Islam, who lived through the centuries, from the eighth century to the present times have been brought together on a common platform.

When I presented this idea in a somewhat sketchy form in three articles, published in *The Illustrated Weekly of India* (dated January 15, 22 & 29, 1989) under the heading: *The Trial,* its editor, Mr. Pritish Nandy, described it as an allegory. I have struggled hard to find a more appropriate word but allegory seems to fill the bill better than any other. *The Shorter Oxford English Dictionary of Historic Principles* describes an allegory as "description of a subject under the guise

X

of another subject of aptly suggestive resemblance." *The Penguin Word Master Dictionary* refers to it as a story, in which "the characters and events have a symbolic, especially moral meaning".

It is true that an allegory is a narration in either the form of poetry or prose, with a double meaning. In this trial also, it is not Benazir, as such who is in the dock, though her presence adds to the significance of the issues in dispute, but the modern Muslim woman who is besieged from within as well as without. In explaining the purport of an allegory, J.A. Cuddon in *A Dictionary of Literary Terms*, cites the old Arab fable of the frog and the scorpion, both of whom wanted to cross the river Nile. They reached an agreement. The frog would carry the scorpion on his back and the scorpion would not sting him, provided the frog would not drown the scorpion. However, true to his nature, the scorpion stung the frog on the way. "Why did you break the agreement", asked the frog as it was about to die. "Because", replied the scorpion, "we are both Arabs". Commenting on this oft-quoted story, Mr. Cuddon comments, "If we substitute for the frog a 'Mr. Treachery' or a 'Mr. Two-Face' and make the river any river and substitute for 'We're both Arabs...' 'We are both men..', we can turn the fable into an allegory.

The *Trial of Benazir* differs from Bunyan's *Pilgrims Progress*, which is the best known allegory in the English language, in the sense that in Bunyan's book, the figures and places are not real but invented by the author, while in this book, the persons are real, their words too are more or less authentic, but their appearance, cutting across time and space, is imaginary.

There are different kinds of allegories, most of which deal with religious subjects; the Old and the New Testament are full of them. So are the stories in the Quran. Plato has also made use of one type of allegory in his *Timaeus, Phaednus* and *Symposium;* some others have used different types. In our times, many of the poems of Iqbal also have allegorical structure.

Some critics may not consider *The Trial of Benazir* strictly allegorical; it is, in fact, part fact, part fiction. Perhaps more fact than fiction as it tries to project the centuries-old controversy on the status of woman in religious and historical terms through proceedings in a court. The persons, whether the petitioners or the respondent, the witnesses or the judges, are real, but their presence in this trial is imaginary.

My object has been to project the various viewpoints of persons, who are revered and respected by the faithful and thus to remove the cobwebs that still exist in the minds of Muslims and non-Muslims alike in respect of the status of woman in Islam. The matter is, indeed, complex but the more light is thrown, the simpler it becomes. Through this trial, in which both sides have stated their case without any reservation, a clearer picture, has hopefully emerged; the trial is just the pretext; the exposition is the real intent.

My wife, Fatma with her vast editorial experience in *The Times of India* group of publications, has scanned every word with her penetrating eye; she has literally burnt the midnight oil working on the manuscript over and over again. If not for her unassuming nature and her insistence on remaining in the background, her name. should, in all fairness, have appeared as co-author of this book. Her contribution in this effort as in every other literary venture of mine, has been invaluable. Words are not adequate to acknowledge my deep sense of gratitude to her.

Bombay
15th August, 1989

SECTION
I

The Case
Before
the Tribunal

1

Introduction

GENERAL Zia-ul-Haq (1924-1988) ruled Pakistan for eleven years (1977-88) with an iron hand. He drew his power from the barrel of a gun. However, in order to give a popular appeal to his martial law administration, he introduced one Islamic measure after another. His advisors were Abu ala Maududi (1903-1979) and his colleagues in the Jamaat·i·Islami, an organisation founded in 1941 which became, in course of time, the premier fundamentalist organisation in South Asia.

Zia had ousted Zulfiqar Ali Bhutto (1928-1979), the popularly elected Prime Minister and his party, the Pakistan People's Party (PPP), from power in 1977; he was thereafter determined to completely eradicate Bhutto's political influence. He therefore harassed the PPP workers, jailed many of them and prosecuted their leader for conspiracy in the case of a murder. The trial dragged on for two years and finally, the Supreme Court of Pakistan held Bhutto guilty by a majority verdict (5:4) and ordered him to be hanged. Doubts were expressed in many legal circles throughout the world about the verdict being misconceived and amounting to judicial murder. Many heads of government appealed to Zia for commuting the death sentence but Zia did not relent. Bhutto was hanged on April 4, 1979.

Benazir (b. 1953), is the eldest daughter of the executed Bhutto; he gave her the best modern education both at Harvard in America and at Oxford in England. Being the favourite among his two sons and two daughters, Benazir received special attention of her father. He saw a spark in her; he felt she had the makings of a leader. Thus she was trained in politics. She was good in her studies and also took active part in students' activities. She was elected to the most coveted post of President of the famed Oxford Union. The hurly burly of politics however did not interest her much; in fact it somewhat unnerved her; she preferred to be a diplomat or a civil servant. But the harrowing ordeals that she, her mother, her sister and her two brothers suffered during the trial of Zulfiqar Ali Bhutto and later, on his execution, steeled her; she turned rebellious, seething with rage and determined to avenge her father's death. She vowed that she would not let her father's murderers rest in peace.

Benazir, in collaboration with her mother Nusrat, began to organise the workers in the PPP to mount an active opposition to Zia whose regime had unleashed terror against all those opposed to him. There was hardly a political party in Pakistan which supported the martial law and approved of Zia's dictatorial methods. Soon after the death of Zulfiqar Ali Bhutto, Nusrat Bhutto became President of the PPP but the moving force behind the struggle was Benazir; both mother and daughter were therefore tortured by the regime for over nine years, imprisoned several times and even exiled. But their sufferings endeared them even more to the people; hence when Benazir returned from London to Pakistan in 1986 after the martial law was lifted by Zia, she was greeted at the Lahore airport with an unprecedented and an almost hysterical welcome. People had poured into the city the night before and thronged all the public places; they greeted her jubilantly — even the policemen waved out to her and cheered her. Delirious workers of the PPP shouted: "Welcome, daughter of Pakistan"; and "Benazir, the harbinger of revolution". They had come from all over Pakistan — Punjab, Sind, Baluchistan and the North-West Frontier Province. They had travelled by wagons, buses, trucks, trains and cars. Dressed in a black linen *kurta,* holding the PPP tricolour flag aloft, Benazir emerged from the plane as an angel of hope; she mounted the truck that awaited her and stood there, tall and stately, responding to the sea of humanity that surrounded her; it was the same story all along the route. She spoke to the people stopping incessantly on the wayside, as her caravan inched its way forward, assuring them that she would not rest content until the dictator had been brought down. The spot reporter of the leading newspaper *Dawn* of Karachi observed:

"The cameras could not capture it all, nor can all the superlatives in the dictionary. I will, therefore, use humble words. I have not seen anything like it before. Benazir Bhutto had the city at her feet, the moment she landed at the Lahore airport.

"The night before her arrival, we were discussing how large a crowd she would attract. I told a friend working with a Gulf newspaper that I expected something like 1,50,000. I have never been wider of the mark. I don't know where they came from but they were there. They were there at the airport, they were there at the Fortress Stadium, they were there on the Mall all day and they were there at Data Sahib's mausoleum. And above all, they were at the Iqbal Park in more numbers than you could count.

"They had come from all over the country. Even Mr. Bhutto had not commanded crowds half as big, at the height of his popularity. She took almost ten hours to reach the Iqbal Park from the airport, waving at the crowds constantly, a gruelling exercise in itself, followed by a 65-minute address in which she used what cricket commentators call, 'controlled aggression'.

"Thanks to the atrocious public address system at the Iqbal park, Ms. Bhutto was not heard by a vast majority of the milling multitudes. That made no difference. Words were not necessary; it was, as she said, an *awami* or a people's referendum, and she knew she had won it. She didn't have to make any promises. Her presence was promise enough".

To the millions, who had gathered, what she said and how she said it — she is no great orator — truly did not matter for what they saw in her, was the hope for the realisation of a dream — that of return of democracy to Pakistan.

Such was the impact of this slender, seemingly fragile but daring, resolute and vivacious young woman on the multitudes, comprising young and old, men and women, wor-

kers and peasants, that it caused widespread tremors
throughout the length and breadth of Pakistan, shaking
everyone in Zia's establishment to his very roots. The dictator was stunned at the massive response; so were the Ulama, the learned theologians, who had declared her a heretic
and believed that she would be heckled, mocked at, and
even stoned by the faithful. They were shocked that instead
of the brickbats, she had been showered with flowers.

After Lahore, Benazir visited other cities of Pakistan;
everywhere the response was the same. Millions of people,
dancing with joy, greeted her and demanded the ouster of
Zia. In Peshawar, the fortress of orthodoxy, where women
are mostly veiled and rarely come out of their homes, men
came in their thousands to see and hear Benazir — unveiled, modern and barely in her early thirties — giving up
their centuries old prejudice against the leadership of. a
woman. In her speech, Benazir assured the male-
dominated Pathan society:

"People think I am weak because I am a woman. Do they
not know that I am a Muslim woman and that Muslim
women have a heritage they can well be proud of ? I have
the patience of Bibi Khadija, the wife of the Prophet (peace
be upon him). I have the perseverance of Bibi Zainab, the
sister of Imam Husain. And I have the courage of Bibi
Aisha, the Prophet's youngest wife, who rode her own
camel into battle at the head of the Muslim army. I am the
daughter of martyr Zulfiqar Ali Bhutto, the sister of martyr
Shah Nawaz Khan Bhutto and I am your sister as well. I
challenge my opponents to meet me on the field of democratic elections."

At the end of her speech, Benazir cried out 'Zia zal'; zal in
Phustu means 'go' and the people shouted in one voice,
zal, zal, zal.' The more Benazir moved among the people,
the more enthusiastic was the peoples' response; each city
and every village vied with one another in giving a more
tumultuous welcome to their new messiah. How did this
happen despite the ceaseless indoctrination by the Government controlled media, branding Benazir as a westernised
woman who was going against the basic tenets of Islam?
No one could explain it. The American magazine, News-

week commented:

"Benazir Bhutto is a study in contradictions. She is an aristocrat by birth, a socialist by conviction and a people-power revolutionary out of sheer necessity. She is a democrat who appeals to feudal loyalties. She is a beautiful young woman who will allow no romance into her life — a politician in purdah. She is an expensively educated, westernised woman who intends to rule a male-dominated, Islamic society. Now, after Radcliffe and Oxford, after prison in Pakistan and exile in London, Bhutto 33 — 'Pinky' to her friends — is home again, planning to topple a government that overthrew, and then hanged the father she adored".

Would she succeed in her mission? The people were with her, but some of her own party leaders, most of the other opposition stalwarts, and nearly every power broker was suspicious of her. The main reason for their hostility was her sex. She told Donna Foote of *Newsweek:* "The people who resent me do so because I am a woman, I am young and I am a Bhutto. Well, the simple answer is, it doesn't matter that I'm a woman, it doesn't matter that I'm young and it is a matter of pride that I'm a Bhutto."

Neither sex nor age have proved to be a handicap for her; in fact these have only added to her charisma. This was easily seen when she returned to Larkana, her ancestral village in the province of Sind, after the successful tour of different parts of Pakistan; most of those who came out to greet her were frenzied young men, jostling with each other, just for a glimpse of their heroine-leader. The impact on them was hypnotic; she played upon them like a maestro, forceful and magnetic; her eyes blazing out of her flushed face, haloed with the black dupatta wrapped round her head and her slender hands slicing the air, she asked: "Are you with me"? And they replied in a frenzy, "Yes, yes, yes". Then she said, "People say I am a young girl, all alone without the protection of father or brother. But aren't you my brothers? Won't you protect me"? And they replied, with greater frenzy, "Yes, yes, yes".

Strangely, Benazir has often confided to her friends that she never wanted to be in politics: "I was scared of politics. I

remember the hushed voices, the grownups talking about
the guns and the shots that were fired — politics was
fearful, politics was bad, politics could lead to death". This
was before her father was overthrown and before he was
hanged; the grim tragedy changed her attitude completely.
She then vowed to avenge the injustice done to her father
and the wrong done to Pakistan and to see that the dictators
and the mullahs would no more ruin and destroy her country's magnificent structure so assiduously built by Quaid-i-
Azam Jinnah and shielded with his life by her father.

It was, no doubt, an uphill task for her — more so in a
male-dominated Muslim environment where Zia had rob-
bed women of every vestige of freedom; they were, once
again, reduced to the status of being slaves to men. And the
mullahs, in the name of Islam, justified every measure Zia
took against women, which deprived them of the very
rights they had gained under Islam. How could she over-
come these obstacles? The list of those ranged against her
was formidable: Apart from the military, the police, the
bureaucrats and the politicians of the Zia establishment
who opposed her with the solid support of the Jamaat-i-
Islami and the other fundamentalist organisations, even
the leaders of the various opposition parties were not in
favour of the leadership of a woman; they feared it would
boomerang on them, it would not get them the votes. Votes
they said, were different from cheers. Benazir stood her
ground; she would not yield the leadership to anyone else,
either to a male senator in the PPP or to someone from any
of the other opposition parties. The young workers were
with her; she discarded the waverers and gathered round
her those who had unflinching faith in her, *despite* her
being a woman. If this was to be the test, she told her
supporters, let it be so; she was confident of the votes and
would not be deterred.

Zia and his allies – both political and religious – realised
that the only weapon that could be used against her was
Islam. On May 29, 1988, Zia suddenly dissolved his hand-
picked Parliament, dismissed Prime Minister Junejo and
called for elections; it was an unexpected development
which took everyone by surprise. People danced in the

street with joy; they looked forward to a new era of democracy. Zia was desperate; he did not so much mind a popularly elected government; but not that of Benazir; he played his last card: the installation of Shariah (the canonical law of Islam as put forth in the Quran) as the supreme law of the land. It was a strange enactment; its provisions were neither properly defined nor were their implications worked out. No guidelines were given; under it any citizen could challenge an existing provision, whether legal or constitutional as "un-Islamic" before any Shariah court and if it was found contrary to the Shariah, it could be struck down. Benazir was apprehensive; as she has observed in her autobiography, *Daughter of the East:*

"Many thought that the timing of Zia's latest exploitation of Islam was directed at me. The Urdu press speculated that Zia could use the interpretation of Islamic bigots and try and prevent me, a woman, from standing for election, or he could use it subsequently to try and disqualify me as the leader of the victorious party in the National Assembly." The religious leaders hinted at the possibility of such a move, so did her other political detractors. Undeterred by it, Benazir mobilised her supporters and plunged into the whirlwind of electoral politics.

Although nervous and no longer sure of his own position, Zia still hoped that the people of Pakistan would not favour Benazir, a woman, as head of government; when questioned by Melinda Liu of *Newsweek* he replied, "If the people choose her, nobody can stop it. but I think it will take a little more time. Benazir's present popularity should not be taken as a guarantee that she is the future Prime Minister of Pakistan".

The first step Benazir took soon thereafter was to challenge Zia's 1985 Voters Registration Act in the Supreme Court under which a political party could be debarred by the Government-appointed Election Commissioner on the vague ground that it was against Islam. This was obviously directed against Benazir and the PPP. The Supreme Court upheld Benazir's plea and declared that no party, registered or unregistered, could be prevented from participating in elections and further that elections in a parliamentary system had to be held on the basis of political parties. The judgement was a shot in the arm for Benazir; it galvanised the PPP too. She toured the country from one end to the other; everywhere the turnout was massive despite the searing heat. Meanwhile, there were rumours that she was in the family way; someone asked her for the truth. She replied, "Even if I am, so what? There is too much at stake to rest".

Under the Constitution, the elections should have been scheduled for August 1988, but Zia put them off by two months. Again, doubts began to disturb Benazir; was Zia serious about holding the elections or would he cancel them at the eleventh hour on some pretext or the other? Later, it transpired that the postponement was due to the news of Benazir's pregnancy: Zia's men had announced the new dates on the basis that Benazir was due to deliver the baby sometime in November. Hence the provincial elections were fixed for November 16, and the National elections for November 18. This, they were confident would make it extremely difficult for her to campaign. However, as luck would have it, the baby pre-empted them; he was born more than a month before the scheduled date.

The election campaign was on in full swing when suddenly fate intervened and changed the entire complex of Pakistani politics. On August 17, 1988, Zia died in an air crash when a Pakistan Air Force C-130 Hercules transport plane hurtled down into the waters of Bahawalpur. This immediately catapulted Benazir to centre stage; while other leaders were still working out alliances and strategies, she promptly embarked on a campaign trail, which enhanced not only her popularity but also her image. During the campaign, Benazir showed maturity in thinking, adroitness in planning and a capacity to make the right move at the right time; she promised to fight the prevailing culture of crime and corruption and give a better life to the poverty-stricken peasants and workers. She was confident that her party would end ethnic strife, secessionist pulls, heroin-smuggling, gun-running and those oppressive measures which were falsely taken in the name of Islam. And the people believed her. The Islamic fundamentalists and her political opponents, gathered under the banner of *Islami Jamhoori It tehad*(Islamic Democratic Alliance), warned the faithful that Benazir was, in fact, a heretic and that her rule would destroy the Islamic edifice of Pakistan. Through banners, posters, pamphlets and slogans, the canard was spread among the religious-minded electorate of Pakistan. Benazir was not perturbed. In an interview to *The Times*, London, she explained her stand:

"What is Zia's Islamisation all about? It boils down to two issues — the amputation of hands and the stoning of people in certain cases. Yet Zia himself knew that there was no consensus for this. And therefore, despite these laws having been passed, there have been very few instances either of amputation or of stoning. What Zia did was not so much in substance...

"Apart from enacting these and some laws which are discriminatory and must be removed, what he actually did was to create a climate of hysteria within the country which made it very difficult for working women, minorities and even those sects which did not concur with the official interpretation of Islamic laws.

"(She turns around to one of her lieutenants to ask a question:) 'Zaid, can you tell me what else he did because I have been racking my brain and I can't see what there was apart from a lot of rhetoric?' ('It was all propaganda', says Zaid).

"Because he couldn't justify military repression, he tried to cloak it in the name of religion and the consequence was the brutalisation of our society."

The results of the elections came as an eye-opener to the world, which had believed Pakistan to be the citadel of Islamic fundamentalism; in province after province, the leaders of the Jamaat-i-Islami were trounced; many candidates lost their deposits; despite the handicaps and restrictions under which Benazir and her PPP worked, they triumphed in every province. In Sind, they won a landslide victory; in Punjab, they secured 53 seats against their rival's 44; in the North-West Frontier and Baluchistan, their alliance partners scored. But even so, majority eluded her in the National Assembly; her party secured 93 seats while her opponents managed to win 54. The rest were won by candidates either of friendly parties or independents, many of whom promised to back her for Prime Ministership. To begin with, the Acting President, Ghulam Ishaq Khan, a protege of Zia, did not call her to form the Government; tension began to mount against the President's ambivalent attitude, even America and Britain on whom Pakistan depended for massive military and economic aid, expressed their protest through the diplomatic channels and through their press. All were agreed that the popular verdict had to be honoured. After prevaricating for almost a week, Ghulam Ishaq Khan finally invited Benazir to take the oath of office as Prime Minister. He praised her as a "young, educated, cultured and talented lady, who had the best qualities of leadership and the foresight of a statesman". This was high tribute from the most unexpected quarter! The new Army Chief, Mirza Aslam Beg, also pledged his loyalty to the Prime Minister.

In a countrywide broadcast on the national television hook-up, Benazir declared, "You have bestowed a great honour on your sister and placed a heavy responsibility on her shoulders. We are standing on the brink of disaster, but a whole generation is ready to launch on constructive efforts to save the country. We will bring an end to hunger and degradation. We shall provide shelter over the heads of the homeless."

This was however easier said than done. Benazir faced, enormous problems: poverty was rampant, unemployment endemic; three out of four Pakistanis were illiterate; the economy was on the verge of bankruptcy; population was rising at the rate of 3.1 per cent. To worsen the situation, the entanglement with the Afghan war had opened an international market for smuggling American-imported arms and weapons meant for the *mujahedeen*; defence expenditure continued to mount. Benazir could not antagonise the generals and alienate the armed forces; her mandate was limited; she had to function with great caution.

Moreover, the Ulama refused to reconcile to her appointment as Prime Minister; they persisted in their contention that a woman could not be the head of an Islamic government. Even the Jamaat-i-Ulama-i-Pakistan, a long-time partner of the PPP, announced its opposition to her rule on religious grounds. On February 27, 1989, more than 500 Ulama from different parts of Pakistan, representing all the schools of Sunni theology (from Deobandis and Brelvis to Ahl Hadis and Wahabis) met in Rawalpindi under the auspices of the *Mutahida (United) Ulama Convention.* They unanimously passed a resolution, calling upon the people to reject her leadership. They vowed that they would not rest content until this anti-Islamic act was undone. Only the Shias differed; their leader, Allama Sajid Ali, Chief of the *Tehrike Nifaze Fiqah-e-Jaffria,* categorically stated that the Shias were not opposed to a woman's rule and advised the Ulama not to embark on a course of action which would, once again, upset the political equilibrium. The intellectuals and the feminists retaliated against the Ulama by declaring that Islam did not allow the Ulama or the Mullahs to dabble into politics; they should mind their own business. The atmosphere became tense and charged with uncertainty.

Politically, Benazir is, today, well entrenched; but her opponents and detractors continue to confront her on the religious front challenging her appointment as Prime Minister of Pakistan on the ground that a woman having been ordained by the Quran, as inferior to man, cannot function as a ruler under the Shariah.

2

The Shariah and the Seven Imams

SHARIAH is an Arabic word; literally it means the path. For the Muslims, it represents the law of Islam. It includes the Quranic injunctions; the Hadith or sayings of the Prophet and the Sunnah, the way or manner in which the Prophet acted or performed. The two words, Hadith and Sunnah often cause confusion. The word, Hadith, means a narrative or communication in general; it refers to a record of sayings of the Prophet; while Sunnah means precedent or custom and implies the concrete action taken by the Prophet in a particular situation. The distinction is quite subtle; scholars have written tomes on it, making confusion worse confounded. To understand the rules and practices derived from these sources, classical jurists have, since the passing away of the Prophet, resorted to certain methods; these include, *inter-alia, ijtihad* or independent thinking, *qiyas* or analogical deductions and *ijma* or consensus of the learned. The jurists were aided in their task by commentators of the Quran and the recorders of the Hadith or traditions. Unfortunately,the rulers made use of the theologians to give wrong interpretations of the Quranic verses and to concoct spurious Hadith to suit their purpose. This resulted in a glut of wrong interpretations and concocted Hadith. The Shariah, or the Islamic set of rules and regulations, degenerated into legal chaos.

To rescue the faith from the morass into which it had fallen,there emerged in the world of Islam, seven religious luminaries, whose combined efforts gave shape, discipline and system to the Shariah. They are the founders of the four schools of theology and jurisprudence — Imam Abu Hanifa, Imam Malik, Imam Shafi'i and Imam Hanbal; the two traditionists — Imam Bukhari and Imam Muslim and finally the restorer of the faith — Imam Ghazali. I have chosen these eminent men to constitute the Supreme Shariah Council for the trial of Benazir Bhutto. They are representatives of the Sunni sect and not the Shia, the petitioners being Sunnis and Benazir, also a Sunni. Thus the law applicable to this case has to be Sunni. The Sunnis believe that succession to leadership of the faithful is by popular choice, the Shias claim that it is through the direct descendants of the Prophet.

Given below are brief accounts of each of the seven Imams revered by the Sunnis:

1.   **Abu Abdullah Muhamed Ibn Ismail**, better known as Imam Bukhari, (810-870) was born at Bukhara in Central Asia. He was a precocious child, attracted to the Hadith or traditions of the Prophet from an early age. In search of knowledge he went on a pilgrimage to Mecca at the age of sixteen. He studied at Medina and then travelled to Egypt and the other parts of the Arab world. He collected more than seven hundred thousand Hadith but then, by applying the strictest rules of reliability and accuracy, rejected all except some seven thousand. These constitute his *Sahih* or true compilation which is regarded by the Sunnis, as the most *authentic* book of traditions. It is held as sacred, next only to the Quran. Bukhari died in Bukhara, where his mausoleum has become a place of pilgrimage for the faithful.

2.   **Abul Husain Asakir-ud-Din Muslim**, better known as Imam Muslim (817-875) was a diligent scholar. Like his master, Imam Bukhari, he also travelled widely all over the Muslim world to collect Hadith. He rejected most of what he collected and compiled in his *Sahih* only those, which fulfilled his tests which were somewhat different from those of his master. The introduction he wrote for his compilation is a masterpiece of Hadith literature. Bukhari subdivided the Hadith under different heads, thus providing a system of rules for jurisprudence. Muslim concentrated more on going to the root of each Hadith rather than bothering about their legal implications. In a way, his work is a complete survey of Muslim theology and hence regarded as

sacred by the Sunnis, next only to the *Sahih* of Imam Bukhari.

3.   **Abu Hanifa Al-Numan ibn Thabit** (700-767) was the founder of the Hanafi School of Law, which today has the largest following of almost 80 percent from among the Sunnis. He is regarded as *Imam-i-Aazam* or the "Greatest Imam". He was a Persian, born in Kufah in Iraq. Abu Hanifa refused the office of Chief Justice offered by several Caliphs and was imprisoned for defying the Caliphal orders. He was not a lawyer, nor a jurist, but a perceptive scholar, who tried to build on scientific principles, a legal system, which could answer every conceivable question of the faithful. He did not lean much on the Hadith or traditions of the Prophet but relied on the Quranic texts and developed his theories around them. He was more for equity than legalism and since he was liberal and humane in his outlook, he went by practical considerations. He did not leave behind any legal code, but his teachings were formalised by two of his distinguished disciples — Qadi Abu Yusuf, who became the Chief Justice under Caliph Harun al-Rashid, and, Muhammad. Some of Abu Yusuf's legal subtleties are reflected in the well-known Arabic work: the *Thousand and One Nights*. The Hanafis are spread all over South and South-east Asia.

4.   **Abu Abd Allah Malik Ibn Anas** (716-795), the founder of the Maliki School of Law, was born in Medina, he also died there. He favoured the historical approach to the Shariah and derived its rules from the local customs of Medina. He was also a practical jurist and concentrated on finding solutions to problems as they arose in the day-to-day life. He often went beyond the Quranic text and the Prophetic usages and strived for an agreed solution based on commonsense. Being in the direct line of the apostolic succession, his eminence was never questioned. He relied on the Hadith but gave them his own interpretations. These were unquestionably followed by his followers. He looked at every question from the point of view of *istislah* or public interest and *maslah* or public advantage. Though he also expounded the doctrine of *ijma* (concensus), it was limited to the Ulama of Medina because for Malik the world did

not extend beyond the City of the Prophet. His book *Mu-watta* (The Path Made Smooth), is the earliest collection of the Hadith and the first book of Islamic law. His followers are mostly in the Arab West and in some parts of Egypt.

5.   **Muhammad Ibn Idris ash-Shafi'i** (767-820), is the real architect of the systematisation of Islamic law. He was born in Palestine but lived mostly in Mecca. He came from the tribe of Quraish to which the Prophet belonged. He studied theology in Medina and pursued higher studies in Baghdad. Unlike Abu Hanifa, with his rationalism, ash-Shafi'i swore by the Hadith and the Sunnah. According to him these were the best sources of interpreting the Quranic injunctions. They were more important than *qiyas* (analogy) or *ijma* (consensus). He placed the *usul al-fiqh* or the rules of jurisprudence in the following order: first the Quran; second, the Hadith and the Sunnah; third, *qiyas* or analogy; and fourth, *ijma* or consensus. Like Abu Hanifa, ash-Shafi'i also did not found any school; that was done by his disciples. He had a keen mind and was endowed with a balanced approach and a clear vision. He could grasp fully the complexities of a problem and discover the means to get to the right solution; he made it clear that "if you find a tradition from the Prophet saying one thing and a decision from me saying another, follow the tradition"; but the tradition had to be absolutely authentic. Shafi'i possessed an extremely logical mind but sometimes he lost his way in the jungle of logic. The Shafi'is live mainly in Egypt; the world famous al-Azhar, the thousand-year-old centre of Sunni theology at Cairo, has been under their influence for centuries. Shafi'is also live in different parts of India, Pakistan and Bangladesh; they predominate in Malaysia and Indonesia.

6.   **Ahmad Ibn Hanbal** (780-855) studied and lectured in Baghdad. He was not a lawyer or a philosopher, but a scholar, who devoted himself to the pursuit of theology. His work, *Masnad*, is a collection of thirty thousand Hadith, rather loosely put together. He was a stickler for form and refused to compromise to appease even a Caliph. He openly defied the Abbasid Caliph, al Mamun and was first imprisoned and then publicly flogged. A man of convic-

18 THE TRIAL OF BENAZIR

tion, he stuck to his views. He was respected by the Muslims of his generation for learning and piety and was venerated as a saint. His emphasis was on strict adherence to the Quranic tenets and injunctions and to purity of life and high moral behaviour. His followers swear by orthodoxy and assert that spiritual truths cannot be reached by worldly wisdom. They are the forerunners of the Wahhabis, the followers of Mohammed Abdul Wahhab of Saudi Arabia who is the mentor of the present day Islamic fundamentalists. Most Saudi Arabians are Hanbalis.

7. **Abu Hamid Muhammad al-Ghazali** (1058-1111) was the great reconciler, who successfully composed the differences among the various schools and sects. His place in Islamic theology is unique. He was, as Ibn Rushd, the great scientist-philosopher of Moorish Spain said, "everything to everyone". Although he was younger than the other six Imams, he has been selected here to head the Supreme Shariah Council, because he had the uncanny capacity of harmonising divergent and sometimes even contradictory viewpoints. No one else could bring the Sufis or the mystics and the puritans or the orthodox together. He was, at once, a philosopher, a theologian, a jurist and a mystic. He was known in Europe as "Algazel" and was highly admired for his genius. He was born in Tus, in Persia; he also died there. An extraordinary figure, Imam Ghazali is regarded as the rejuvenator of Islam. He is called *Hujjatul Islam* or the "Proof of Islam". A prolific writer, he wrote more than seventy books, explaining his pursuit for truth. He wrote, "I arrived at the truth, after a prolonged search, not by reasoning or accumulating proofs, but through a flash, which God in His wisdom, sent into my soul". He did not give much weight to reason. He believed that, "where faith enters, reason departs". That is why in his later life he was drawn more and more towards Sufism, although he affirmed that Muslims could not do without the exoteric framework of law and theology in their day-to-day life. He told his critics that "to refute you must first understand". He studied all theologies and the viewpoint of every school; he even paid heed to what his worst detractors said and then tried to make the best out of the given situation. Thus he

was able to synthesise orthodoxy, theology, law and mysticism and take Islam out of the chaos in which he found it. His contribution to religious values and practices is, indeed, invaluable. He came as a breath of fresh air and freed Islam from the entanglements of contradictory forces, bringing the faithful under a unified pattern. He did not strike out a new path instead he blazed a new light on the trodden one and made it a common highway for the ordinary Muslims. He is venerated as much as the founders of the four schools and the two great traditionists.

The proceedings of the trial of Benazir Bhutto before this Council follow; these are, no doubt, imaginary but through them much light is thrown on the complexities of man-woman relationship in Islam. No aspect is left untouched; no question, unanswered. The trial is fictional; but the various viewpoints presented therein are more authentic than fictional. That is what makes the trial allegorical — a mixture of fact and fancy.

SECTION
II

Who Is
a Muslim?

3

The Petition

First Day

A S soon as the news about the petition against Benazir Bhutto, Prime Minister of Pakistan, was made
public, the Muslim world was agog with specula-
tion. Would she continue in office? None could tell. The
petitioners were the Ulama of the highest ranks; their leader was the eminent Muslim savant of the subcontinent,
Maulana Sayyid Sulaiman Nadvi. The other petitioners
included such learned theologians as Maulana Sayyid Abul
ala Maududi, Mufti Muhammad Shafi, Mujtahid Jaffar
Hussain, Maulana Ihteshamul Haq, Pir Muhammad Amin
al Hasanat, Qadi Abdus Samat Sarbazi, Maulana Sayyid
Muhammad Daud Guaznavi and others. They had requested that the Supreme Shariah Council declare the election
of Benazir Bhutto as head of Government, ultra vires the
Shariah. As a result, there was intense interest all round;
even non-Muslim countries followed the event keenly.

The venue selected for the Council was the great hall of
the world-famous Al-Azhar, the thousand-year-old stron-
ghold of Sunni theology at Cairo, built by the Shia Fatimid
rulers in 972. Its campus has a magnificent mosque and
several stately buildings, built by successive Egyptian rulers. On the fall of the Fatimids, the Sunni Ayyubids trans-
formed it from a Shia centre of theology into one of Sunni
orthodoxy and research. Students came to it from far and
near; with the passage of time, its fame spread. It reached
its peak under the rectorship of Shaikh Muhammad Abduh, the Chief Qadi of Egypt. During the rule of Nasser it
was brought under government control; even so, its religious eminence has remained undiminished. Sunni Islam
looks to it for guidance.

President Hosni Mubarak of Egypt had made elaborate arrangements for the occasion. He had also taken special care to provide gracious hospitality to the many learned theologians, scholars and public figures, who were arriving in Cairo to attend and, if necessary, to participate in the proceedings.

The hall of Al-Azhar looked spectacular; chandeliers adorned the majestic,high-domed ceiling,exquisite Iranian carpets with Quranic verses, woven in extraordinary crafts-manship, hung on the walls. It was an imposing setting; historic figures from Islam's past and present had assem-bled; each of them exuded awe – some with their spiritual aura and some with worldly dignity. In fact such a galaxy of the great, who lived at different periods, from the eighth century to the present times, coming together in one place had itself evoked tremendous public interest the world over. At the gates and inside the hall were the Egyptian guards, clad in scarlet and black uniforms with multi-coloured turbans wrapped round their heads and swords of shining brass and steel strapped to their sides.

At the appointed hour, the most Hon'ble Imams, consti-tuting the Supreme Shariah Council, headed by Imam Gha-zali, entered the hall; one by one they took their seats on the dais especially erected for the purpose. The clerk of the Council, the Syrian scholar, Rashid Rida (1865-1935), who had achieved great fame as editor of *al-Mannar*, Cairo, announced their arrival and the entire gathering stood up in reverence. Then Rida asked A.K. Brohi (1915-1987), the well-known lawyer and Islamic scholar, who had been the Attorney General and the Law Minister of Pakistan, whe-ther he was ready with his case. He was appearing on behalf of Sayyid Sulaiman Nadvi(1884-1953) and the forty Ulama of Pakistan, who, in a convention, had opined that the head of an Islamic State had to be a Muslim male.

On behalf of Benazir Bhutto, the respondent, was the Rt. Hon'ble Mr. Ameer Ali (1849-1928), an eminent Indian jurist, whose book *The Spirit of Islam* has become a classic, assisted by Mr. Yahya Bakhtiar, the Attorney-General of Pakistan. The latter had defended Benazir's father, Zulfiqar Ali Bhutto, in the murder case instituted against him by the then Martial Law Administrator Zia-ul-Haq which had resulted in Bhutto's execution.

A.K. Brohi sought the permission of the Council to proceed.

Imam Ghazali: You may also give us the list of the expert witnesses you propose to call.

"Allow me first to state my case my reverend Imam" pleaded Brohi.

"Please go ahead," said Imam Abu Hanifa.

Brohi: The case of the petitioners, who are all highly respected scholars, is that the appointment of Benazir Bhutto, as the amir or head of government, is against the Shariah. They are challenging it on two grounds: one that the lady is not a proper Muslim in the sense that she has violated every known cannon of Islam by her conduct and her style of living; and two, that even if she is held by this reverend and honourable Council to be a proper Muslim, then too, as a woman, she is debarred under the Shariah to be a ruler.

Imam Ghazali: Don't you think it would be better if, to begin with, we proceed with the first issue; in case we uphold your contention that Benazir is not, as you put it, a proper Muslim, then the second issue will not survive and we may not go into it at all?

Brohi: As you wish, Your Honour.

"What do you say", asked Imam Shafi'i of Ameer Ali who was defending Benazir?

Ameer Ali: I have no objection, my Imam. But apart from these issues, there is yet another important matter which is most relevant here, on which I may be permitted to express my views. And that is the general status of woman in Islam. I feel that unless we clear our minds about it, the specific question — whether a Muslim woman can be the ruler of an Islamic state or not–will not make much sense. My contention, my venerable Imams is that the Quran allows no distinction between a male and a female, except in family affairs, and hence the question whether a woman can be a ruler does not arise.

Imam Shafi'i: You have raised an interesting point; so you feel that if we accept your argument then Brohi's main charge against Benazir becomes irrelevant.

Imam Malik: This may open theological floodgates; but, I have no objection to that.

Imam Hanbal: I suppose, in view of the importance of the issues involved, we should hear both sides on the larger question first — that of the status of woman in Islam. Over the centuries, all sorts of innovations have been introduced and it will be better if these are clarified, once for all.

Imam Bukhari: I agree; but why separate the two issues. Are they not interrelated?

Ameer Ali: May I elaborate a little, my Honourable Sirs? Perhaps, I have not made myself properly understood. I am firmly of the opinion that Islam divides human activities into two spheres: one, the family; and two, the outside world. It is because the operation of these two spheres, clearly defined by the Quran, is not understood that there is all this confusion. In fact this has been happening over the centuries. Imam Hanbal is right; the classical jurists have added their own interpretations and put a lot of moss around the Quranic injunctions. It is better if this venerable Council gives clear guidance so that the faithful may not err any longer.

Imam Ghazali: Have you any objection to that, Brohi?

Brohi: None whatsoever. The confusion has been created by persons like my learned friends who have been influenced by the West. They have read meanings in some of the Quranic verses, which I feel are not there; they have interpolated words into them. They are the apologists for Islam, the rootless cosmopolitans as I would call them.

Ameer Ali: I protest, Your Honour; I have done as much, if not more, to serve the cause of Islam as my learned friend.

Imam Abu Hanifa: Please avoid personal aspersions; our Prophet has said: do not look at who is saying but think of what he is saying.

Brohi then presented Maulana Ihtishamul Haq to the Council. The stern-looking but dignified Maulana slowly stepped into the witness box and took the oath placing his hand on the Quran, with his eyes closed and his head lowered in reverence to the Holy Book. In his examination-in-chief, Brohi asked the Maulana, who had been in the forefront of the agitation against Benazir to state his reasons for it to the Council.

Ihtishamul Haq: I am firmly of the opinion that Benazir is not a good Muslim.

Imam Abu Hanifa: That is for Allah to decide.

Ihtishamul Haq: True my reverend Imam, but Allah has set certain guidelines in this respect. Our Prophet prescribed the code of conduct to his followers. My point is that Benazir neither follows those guidelines nor the code of conduct. She is more Christian in her outlook than Islamic, more western than Arab in her mode of life. She cuts her hair short, wears make-up, mixes freely with men and wears no *hijab* or veil. I am sure she does not pray or fast in the month of Ramadan nor gives *zakat* or charity as prescribed in Islam. I don't think she has performed the *hajj* or pilgrimage. What sort of a Muslim is she then? And she is to rule over us! I don't want to go into the shocking details of her life at Harvard and Oxford. The less said about it, the better.

Ameer Ali: I object, Your Honour! This is character assasination. There is no foundation in either fact or law to these allegations. The Maulana has jaundiced eyes; he sees everything yellow in those whom he disagrees with.

Imam Ghazali looked irritated; he asked Brohi dryly whether he had finished with his examination-in-chief of the witness.

Brohi: I will ask one more question: Will you tell the Council, Maulana, whether such a Muslim as you have described can remain within the Islamic fold?

Ihtishamul Haq: No. Benazir is a *munafiq*, a hypocrite. She claims to be a Muslim, but in reality, she is not. The Quran is clear on this point.

Amir Ali got up to cross-examine the Maulana.

Ameer Ali: Will you tell me, Maulana Saheb, where is it written in the Quran that a Muslim has to follow the Arab way of life?

Ihtishamul Haq: (fumbling uncomfortably) The Quran is in Arabic; the Prophet was an Arab. We bear Arabic names;

we say our prayers in Arabic. What you wear, Mr. Ameer Ali, is western; what I wear is Islamic. That is the difference between you and me. Our outward must reflect our inward. We must not only *be* Muslims, we must also *look* Muslims.

Ameer Ali: Do you mean to say that all those Muslims who do not know Arabic or do not follow the Arab way of life are not Muslims?

Ihtishamul Haq: They are not good Muslims. They may be Muslims in name but not in reality.

Ameer Ali: Are you not challenging the universality of Islam? If Muslims everywhere were to look alike, dress alike, talk alike, the diversity which Islam encourages would disappear.

Imam Ghazali: I would like both of you to keep to the point. Please do not digress from the issue in question.

Ameer Ali: May I know from the Maulana which specific verse in the Quran or which Hadith prohibits a Muslim woman from using cosmetics or cutting her hair short?

Ihtishamul Haq: It is all implied; there are enough references but one has to have the insight, born out of learning and piety, to comprehend the teachings of the Quran and the Prophet.

Ameer Ali: So you admit that there is nothing mentioned specifically in the Quran or any book of Hadith; it is all a matter of deduction or rather interpretation.

Ihtishamul Haq: I have nothing in common with my friend; I see no point in arguing with him.

Imam Ghazali asked Brohi to call his next witness. Maulana Abu ala Maududi stepped in.

Brohi: Are you the founder of Jamaat-i-Islami?

Maududi: Yes.

Brohi: With what object did you found it?

Maududi: To establish the Kingdom of God on this earth according to the tenets of Islam.

Brohi: Is it a fact that you had opposed the formation of Pakistan?

Maududi: Yes.

Brohi: Why then have you lived and worked in Pakistan all this while?

Maududi: Because I believed I could help transform it into a Kingdom of God.

Brohi: Do you know that Benazir is a daughter of Pakistan, born on its soil and Pakistani parents?

Maududi: Birth makes no difference; it is the belief that matters.

Brohi: Do you doubt Benazir's belief?

Maududi: I do. She does not practice what she claims to believe. She has never tried to understand the real teachings of the Quran and live upto them. Her father engaged an English governess to teach her; thereafter she was educated in America and England. She may carry a Muslim name but she knows little about Islam. You see, there are two kinds of Muslims among us — the political Muslims and the real Muslims.

Imam Shafi'i: Why should the one exclude the other?

Maududi: According to me they do. One is a *be-amal* Muslim — a Muslim without action; another is a *ba-amal* Muslim — one who practises what he believes in and he is the real Muslim. It is better to have one *ba-amal* Muslim than a thousand *be-amal* ones.

Imam Ghazali: By this criterion you will exclude a large number of Muslims from our fold.

Maududi: Be it so.

In his cross-examination of the Maulana, Ameer Ali asked whether the Quran had given the right to anyone to decide on who was a true Muslim or was it left to Allah alone to judge.

Maududi: I don't follow your question.

Ameer Ali: I will put it differently. If a man has declared that he is a Muslim, can another Muslim take it upon himself to decide whether the person is indeed a Muslim or not? Or what kind of a Muslim he is, good, bad or indifferent. Has he got that right? Or is Allah alone the arbiter?

Maududi: I shall explain, my venerable Imams. Some Muslims profess faith in God and the Prophet and declare Islam as their religion; but then they confine Islam to only part of their lives. Their relations with their wives, children, family and the society are to a great extent unaffected by Islam and are based on secular considerations. As landlords, traders, rulers, soldiers, professionals or people in other spheres of activity, they behave as if they are autonomous, having no connection with their status as Muslims. And since such Muslims are in a majority, the leadership of the community has passed into their hands. But they are rebels against God and his Prophet. God does not desire them; the Prophet does not want them.

Ameer Ali: And it is you, Maulana Maududi, who will decide what God desires and what the Prophet wants?

Maududi: I say this on the basis of their teachings.

Imam Shafi'i: And it is on the basis of your personal opinion that you want Benazir to be out of our fold?

Maududi: That opinion is based on sound foundation; I would treat her as a *munafiq*, a hypocrite and you, my learned Imams, know what should be the fate of a *munafiq* in Islam.

The last witness called by Brohi was Ibn Taimiyya (1263-1328) whose theological treatises have been unsurpassed in the forceful representation of orthodoxy. He propagated the return to the pristine purity of early Islam with rare intellectual courage. He was shocked at the "accretions, innovations and dross" that had gathered around the faith and the misuse of Islamic traditions by the ruling elite. He spoke at first of the moral degeneration of Islam at the hands of power seekers and then pointed out:

"It has been established from the Quran, from the Sunnah and from the general unanimity of our nation that he who forsakes the law of Islam should be fought though he may have once pronounced the two formulas, namely belief in the oneness of God and the prophethood of Muhammad. There may be differences of opinion regarding those who neglect voluntary but established forms of worship However there is no unanimity regarding the duties and prohibitions which are both explicit and obligatory. He who neglects them should be fought until he agrees to abide (by these duties and prohibitions) — to perform the five assigned prayers daily, to pay the *zakat* (alms), to fast during the month of Ramadan, and to undertake Hajj or pilgrimage to the Ka'ba (at Mecca). Furthermore, they should avoid all forbidden acts, like marriage with sisters, the eating of impure foods (such as pork, flesh of cattle that has died or was unlawfully slaughtered), and the attack on the lives and wealth of Muslims. Any such trespasser of the Shariah should be fought, provided that he had knowledge of the mission of the Prophet (peace be upon him). This knowledge makes him responsible to obey'the orders, the prohibitions, and the permits. If he disobeys he should then be fought".

On being cross-examined by Ameer Ali as to why he did not issue any *fatwa* (a judicial opinion or decree) expelling the rulers of his time who did not conform to these prescriptions from the fold of Islam, Ibn Taimiyya's reply was rather evasive "I did the best I could; but my best was not enough," he averred. Ameer Ali did not pursue the matter further.

As Brohi had concluded his list of witnesses, Imam Ghazali turned to Ameer Ali and asked him whether he intended to call any expert witnesses in defence of Benazir. "Yes, my venerable Imams," replied Ameer Ali. "You may proceed then", said Imam Ghazali.

Ameer Ali: My first witness, Your Honour, is Allama Shaikh Muhammad Iqbal (1875-1938), the great poet-philosopher of Islam, who was the first to bring Maududi's writings to the notice of Muslims in undivided India and whose poetry stirred the Muslim world.

Iqbal stepped into the witness box. He swore by the Quran and, in reply to a question by Ameer Ali, said "I have no intention, my Honourable Imams, to pontificate before you; I am a mere poet who loves Islam and the Prophet. I am happy that my poetry had some impact on my co-religionists and has awakened them to a realisation of their glorious heritage. To me, Islam is all-embracing; I do not subscribe to the theory of exclusion. I submit that no Muslim, however good and pious, has a right to declare another Muslim — whatever be his conduct — a *kafir* or a non-believer. According to my understanding of the Quran, a Muslim is one who believes in the two fundamentals of our faith; one, that there is no God but Allah and two, that Muhammad is the last of His Prophets. Once he has made the declaration, then no one can take him out of the fold of

Islam. For his lapses and sins, he is answerable to Allah and to no one else. Our religion recognises no intermediaries between a believer and his Creator".

"Your witness", said Ameer Ali to Brohi.

Brohi turned to Iqbal: I have great regard for your love of Islam Allama Iqbal; but don't you think there has to be some regulation to keep our House of Islam in order?

Iqbal: What has history taught us? Did regulations keep the House in order? The more our scholars and jurists argued, the more our edifice was weakened. Factions grew; sects multiplied. The result was more confusion and chaos. Islam's real strength lies in its simplicity and in its believers having direct communion with God. That is why our Prophet emphasised that he was no more than a messenger; it is the message that matters. And such is the message that it mesmerises a human being. Who are we, pray, to question another person's belief? If he betrays God, God will punish him. He may even forgive him if He so desires. That is the spirit of Islam and the essence of the mission of the Prophet.

The next witness Ameer Ali called was Muhammed Abduh (1849-1905), the eminent Rector of Al-Azhar and the Chief Qadi of Egypt, whose learning has left a deep impress on the Arab world. He said that Muslims should not narrow their approach to their religion; Islam did not consist merely in praying five times, or fasting during Ramadan, or giving zakat or performing hajj. The Quran, he explained, repeatedly emphasised two things; belief in the unity or oneness of God and amlus saleh, right conduct. "Our Prophet", he said, "came as a beacon light of broard humanism; he preached goodwill and tolerance. He told us that Allah was most merciful and kind. Allah himself tells us repeatedly of his compassion. How then can this Council turn itself into a military tribunal and expel persons arbitrarily from its fold, when all Muslims are equal unto one another? That would be a travesty of justice, nay even worse, a betrayal of our faith. Allah is the best of judges; Benazir has declared that she is a Muslim. That is enough. If she is insincere, Allah will know how to deal with her. He knows best; His ways are inscrutable. We cannot meddle in them."

Brohi, while cross-examining Abduh, tried to attack his bonafides by saying that he had compromised with the West, by trying to reform Islam according to western requirements. Such a reformed Islam, he said, would not be Islam.

Imam Ghazali intervened; he asked Brohi to confine his remarks to the issues before the Council and not indulge in personal recriminations. Brohi apologised and continued with his questioning. "Thousands of *fatwas* or decrees have been issued by jurists on this question; is it your contention that they were all wrong?

Abduh: I would not say that, but a *fatwa* is not a final statement; it is, at best, a theological observation. It is not infallible. On this basic question which goes to the root of Islam, I am absolutely uncompromising whatever be the opinion of others.

At this stage a great savant, Ahmad Sirhindi (1564-1624), who had carried on a relentless fight against the religious policy of the Mughal Emperor, Akbar, stood up from the audience and requested to be heard. Silence prevailed as soon as people heard his voice and saw his imposing figure.

Imam Ghazali said that the members of the Council would be happy to hear the views of one, who had carved out an enduring place for himself in the hearts of the Muslims.

"My fellow Imams", spoke Sirhindi, "I do not know much about Benazir or even Pakistan; I have lost interest in the activities of Muslim rulers, ever since they sat in the lap of the Christian West and imitated their ways. To me Islam is complete and final; it needs no reformation. Muslims need not borrow anything from others. However, I put equal emphasis on words and deeds; Akbar, the Mughul Emperor, continued to declare that he was a Muslim; but he did everything against the interests of Islam. I opposed him. Does Benazir fall into that category? I suppose it is too early to say; she has just taken over the reins of an Islamic state. But first, we need to find out if Pakistan is an Islamic state. I do not know. I am not sure. Again, Benazir is not an absolute ruler as Akbar was; but if her past is a guide to her future, then corrective action is certainly called for. What that corrective action should be, it is for this Council to decide. However, I don't agree with those, who have contended here that the community cannot guard itself against wrong elements. It has to help every Muslim to tread the right path. It is better to first try and reform people rather than exclude them from the fold. But if they cannot be corrected, then of course, some action by the community would be called for.

"Well said", said Imam Hanbal. "The Council appreciates the clarity of your thought and the lucidity of your expression."

Imam Ghazali asked Ameer Ali whether he was going to examine Benazir. "I propose to do so later, Your Honour", said Ameer Ali.

The President of the Council held consultations with the other Imams and declared that the Council would like to hear Benazir on her faith in Islam.

Brohi promptly got up and asked, "I hope I shall have the right to cross-examine her?"

"By all means", declared Imam Ghazali.

"And I hope she will be dressed as prescribed in Islam", said Brohi.

"I strongly object to the insinuation", reacted Yahya Bakhtiar angrily. "Benazir respects the Islamic way and is well aware of how to present herself; she is steeped in Islamic culture; she is a much respected lady who has conducted herself with great dignity and has held her own wherever she has gone. She is an ornament to Islam. It does not become my learned friend to speak of her so."

Imam Abu Hanifa cautioned both the sides to show tolerance, which was an essential part of the teachings of Islam.

Imam Ghazali declared that the Council be adjourned for the day; it would meet the next day at the same time.

4

The Preliminary Verdict

Second Day

The Council reassembled and Rashid Rida, the clerk, called out the case. Ameer Ali sought the permission to call Begum Nusrat Bhutto, the mother of Benazir, as a witness. He explained: "Before I put Benazir in the witness box, I would like to examine her mother, since allegations have been made that Benazir was not brought up according to Islamic norms". Imam Ghazali nodded his approval. Nusrat Bhutto, tall and thin, in a white sari, walked gravely upto the witness box and took the oath.

Ameer Ali: Madam, are you a Shiite?

Nusrat Bhutto: Yes.

Ameer Ali: And you married Zulfiqar Ali Bhutto who was a Sunni?

Nusrat Bhutto: Yes.

Ameer Ali: How did you bring up your children?

Nusrat Bhutto: The children followed their father's faith. At the same time I also inculcated in them respect for my faith. Neither my husband nor I felt there was any conflict in this; we were a happy family and there was complete harmony between us.

Ameer Ali: Was this because you had opted for the western way of life and were not bothered about Islamic practices?

Nusrat Bhutto: That is not true. Both our families have been fairly traditional. We were taught all the religious rites and we followed them.

Ameer Ali: What steps did you take to bring up your daughter Benazir as a Muslim?

Nusrat Bhutto: I initiated her personally into the rituals of Islam — she was taught to say her prayers, she fasted along with the rest of the family in the month of Ramadan; when she was a little girl, she learnt to read and recite the Quran from a maulvi engaged by us. He narrated to her the life of the Prophet and explained the fundamentals of Islam. Her father told her stories from the history of Islam. When she grew up he gave her books on Islam and encouraged her to read these books for a better understanding of the religion, the Prophet and his teachings. I took her to religious gatherings; we observed all the customs and followed the tenets of Islam.

Ameer Ali: Will it be right to say that you did everything to bring up Benazir as a good, practising Muslim?

Nusrat Bhutto: Certainly, in fact initially, I also made her wear the veil.

Ameer Ali: Oh! What happened then ? Why did she give it up?

Nusrat Bhutto: My husband did not approve of it; he said it was not necessary as neither the Quran nor the Prophet had prescribed it.

Brohi then cross-examined her "How much time were you able to spend with Benazir when she was growing up?" he asked.

Nusrat Bhutto: Quite a lot, although I wish I could have spent more. I had to accompany my husband who was a minister in Ayub Khan's Cabinet, to various public engagements and we had to go abroad as well.

Brohi: So these engagements took you away from home quite often.

Nusrat Bhutto: Yes.

Brohi: Were not the children then given entirely in the care of Christian governesses?

Nusrat Bhutto: I would not say that; both my husband and I were conscious of our responsibilities to them; we made special arrangements for them to stay with elders of our family while we were away; and we kept in constant touch with them.

Brohi: Can anyone else ever take the place of parents?

Nusrat Bhutto: No, but parents have other responsibilities as well; our job is not only to look after our children, we have also to honour our social and politicial obligations.

Brohi: That may be so as far as the father is concerned.

Nusrat Bhutto (excitedly): No. The woman also has her duties as a wife; she is required to be by her husband's side and assist him in every way. She has also to serve the community to the best of her abilities.

Ameer Ali then called Benazir. The young and beautiful Prime Minister walked serenely towards the witness box; in a **green** *shalwar-kameez* with a white *dupatta*, covering her head, Benazir looked a picture of poise and dignity. She took the oath on the Quran, clearly and in a measured tone.

"In our home, education was given top-priority. My father and before him my grandfather,both wanted to project us as shining examples to the new generation of educated and progressive Pakistanis. At three, I was sent to Lady Jennings' Nursery School, at five to the Convent of Jesus and Mary, which was considered at that time, the best school in Karachi; in school we were taught in English; the language we spoke at home was Urdu although my father's mother tongue was Sindhi and my mother's was Persian.

"I went to a missionary school where we had Irish nuns as our teachers, but no effort was ever made by them to intervene in our religious beliefs and there was never any attempt to try and convert us to the Christian faith."

Ameer Ali: Are you the oldest of the four children of Zulfiqar Ali Bhutto — two sons and two daughters?

Benazir: Yes; one of my brothers died recently under mysterious circumstances.

Ameer Ali: Were the girls in your home given the same kind of education as the boys?

Benazir: Absolutely. My father was very particular about it; my sister and I were given the same opportunities in life as my brothers. At an early age we learnt that Islam made no distinction in this regard; it was men's interpretation of our religion that restricted women's opportunities.

Ameer Ali: What about your religious education?

Benazir: Ever since our childhood, every afternoon we read and learnt by heart, verses from the Quran with the maulvi who came to the house to give us religious instruction. Reading the Holy Quran in Arabic, understanding its meaning and above all, imbibing its essence — this was the most important part of our education at home.

'Paradise lies at the feet of the mother', our maulvi taught us during those daily sessions at home. He cited Quranic injunctions which tell the faithful always to be kind to one's parents and to obey them. He told us that our actions in this world determine our destiny in the afterlife. 'You will have to cross over a valley of fire and the bridge will be as thin as a single strand of your hair', he would say threateningly sending a chill down my spine. 'Those who have sinned here will fall into the fire of hell while those who have done good deeds will cross over to Paradise where streams of milk and honey flow and gardens full of trees of pomogranate and other fruits give cool shelter.'

My mother taught me the ritual of prayers. She took her faith very seriously. No matter where she went, in Pakistan or abroad, no matter how busy she was or what she was doing, when the time came for prayers, she unfailingly turned her face westward, towards Mecca, and prostrated before the Almighty. When I was barely five, I too spread my *Janamaz* (prayer mat) alongside hers and prayed.

Ameer Ali: What kind of religious gatherings did you accompany your mother to?

Benazir: There would be *mawlud* (hymns in adoration of the Prophet for his birthday celebration) and *Quran Khani* (recitation from the Quran) either in our home or in those of our friends and relations. Since my mother is a Shiite, she took me very often to the *majlis* or religious gatherings during the month of Moharrum to hear the maulvi on the significance of the martyrdom of Imam Husain, the grandson of the Prophet. I would sometimes dress in black as she did and go with her to join the other women in the Shiite rituals. These ceremonies interested me as a child for they were more elaborate than those of the Sunnis. I would sit spell-bound as I heard the speakers recapture the tragedy that befell Imam Husain and his small band of followers at Kerbala in Iraq where they were ambushed and brutally slaughtered by the troops of the usurper Caliph, Yazid. No one was spared, not even the little children who fell to Yazid's arrows and swords. Imam Husain was beheaded, his sister Zainab was made to walk bareheaded to Yazid's court where she watched the tyrant play with the head of her brother. But Zainab did not let this break her spirit, instead she became more resolute as did the other followers of Imam Husain. Their descendants, known as the Shiites, even to this day, never let themselves forget the tragedy at Kerbala.

Ameer Ali: Did any particular incident make a deep impact on your mind then?

Benazir: Yes, when I heard the description of the plight of the little baby at Kerbala, crying out for water. The speaker would narrate: 'Hear the little baby cry for water, hear her voice filled with emotion. Feel the heart of the mother hearing the cry of her child. Look at the handsome man, going for the water on horseback. He bends by the river. We can see him bending. Look, there! Men are attacking him with swords ...' As he went on, women in the *majlis* struck their chests in anguish and wailed and wept, performing the *matam* (the mourning). I felt as if my heart would stop beating and I wept and wept.

Ameer Ali: That is all, Your Honour!

Brohi rose to cross-examine Benazir. He got up slowly from his seat and looked intently at Benazir.

Brohi: Have you always prayed five times a day, even when you were studying at Harvard and Oxford? And did you fast religiously during Ramadan?

Benazir: Have I to give an account of my prayers and fasts to my learned friends, my venerable Imams?

Imam Ghazali: Each one to his deeds. Allah alone will take the account. Next question, Brohi.

Brohi: What is the difference between Christianity and Islam. Since, you spent most of your younger days in the West among Christians you must be only too familiar with Christianity. Could you tell us what is the difference between Christianity and Islam?

Benazir: Yes, I have studied under Christian tutors and lived among Christian boys and girls but they genuinely had great respect for the religious beliefs of others. I was born a Muslim and I have always been proud of my Islamic heritage. Even at Harvard and Oxford, I stuck tenaciously to my faith. I was not concerned with Christianity or any other religion. Nor did anyone try to wean me away from my faith. I was happy to be a Muslim and the western environment did not interfere in anyway with my religious beliefs or practices.

Imam Ghazali asked Benazir to step down.

Ameer Ali's last witness, surprisingly, was Hasan al-Banna (1906-1949), the founder of the Muslim Brotherhood, the premier fundamentalist organisation in the Arab world. Fired with religious zeal, al-Banna, a school teacher, became a force in Egypt, attracting large numbers of people to his way of thinking. He preached the rejection of the inroads the West had made in the Islamic edifice and called for a return to the original purity of Islam.

Ameer Ali thanked al-Banna for his cooperation and said that he would not keep him too long. He asked:

"We would like to know your opinion on whether a Muslim who has declared his or her allegiance to Islam can be thrown out of the Islamic fold by any outside agency, however eminent and pious, on the ground that this particular Muslim does not practise what he or she believes in?"

Banna: Non-practising Muslims cannot be any source of strength to Islam; but I don't think they can be thrown out from the community unless they clearly and unambiguously utter the words of rejection of their faith. For instance, if they openly deny the oneness of God, or the prophethood of Muhammad, or if they belie the Quran or commit *Kufr*, (denial of God) then they can of course be expelled. Otherwise, one who utters the *Kalima*, namely belief in the unity of God and the prophethood of Muhammad, continues to be a Muslim, even if he or she is found wanting in the practices of Islam.

Ameer Ali: Thank you, Sir.

Brohi declined to cross-examine Banna and closed his case.

Imam Ghazali asked Benazir to return to the witness box; he asked her whether she had ever entertained any doubt about the beneficence of Islam.

Benazir: No, my reverend Imams, never has such an outrageous thought ever crossed my mind.

Imam Ghazali: Can you tell us what is the basis of our

faith?

Benazir: Belief in the oneness of God and in the Prophet-hood of Muhammed and I believe in it with all my heart. I further believe that our Prophet was the last and the best of all the Prophets of God. I also believe in the Day of Judgement and in all the tenets of Islam. And I affirm that I have done and shall always do my best to live up to them.

Imam Ghazali talked to his colleagues softly and announced a recess for consultation. The members of the Council, dispersed and met in the ante-chamber attached to the hall, where they debated for an hour among themselves. They then returned to the hall. Imam Ghazali informed the distinguished gathering that the Council had authorised him to pronounce its judgement on the point in dispute. He began:

"My most learned colleagues and I are satisfied with Benazir's declaration. On the basis of our understanding of the Quran , we say that no jurist or theologian, however great, has the right to declare a believer to be a non-believer. Whoever asserts to the contrary is himself a non-believer because he denies the prescription of the Holy Book. He constricts the vast mercy of God to His servants and makes Paradise the preserve of a small clique of theologians. He disregards what is handed down to us by the Sunnah; for in the time of the Prophet, may Allah bless and save him, and in the time of the Companions of the Prophet, may God be pleased with them. Islam recognised whole groups of rude Arabs though they worshipped idols. They did not concern themselves with the science of analogical proof and would have understood nothing of it if they had. Whoever claims that theology, abstract proof and systematic classifications are the foundation of belief is an innovator."

Imam Ghazali continued: "Rather, belief is a light which God bestows on the hearts of His creatures as the gift and bounty from Him, sometimes through an explainable conviction from within, sometimes because of a dream in sleep, sometimes by seeing the state of bliss of a pious man and the transmission of his light through association and conversation with him and sometimes through one's own state of bliss".

Imam Hanbal: I agree with the general approach of Imam Ghazali, who has discussed the matter with all of us before pronouncing the judgement; I may however add that whoever among those who pray in the direction of Mecca, dies believing in one God, should be prayed over, and forgiveness asked for his sins. He may not be deprived of the prayer for forgiveness, and we should not neglect to pray for him for any sin that he may have committed, whether it be great or small. It is for God, the Mighty and Glorious to judge him.

Imam Malik: There is a Hadith which has a direct bearing on the issue under dispute; it is reported that Khalid bin Walid, the great warrior of Islam, overpowered a non-believer during a battle and was about to strike a fatal blow, when the non-believer raised his hands and uttered the words: 'There is no god but God and Muhammad is the Prophet of God'. Khalid was not impressed by his recitation of the *Kalima* and killed him instantly. When the Prophet heard about it, he was upset; he asked Khalid for an explanation.

'He obviously recited that only to save his life', Khalid said. 'How do you know' the Prophet asked and added: 'No one except God knows what lies in the heart of man at a particular moment.' Hence a declaration is enough proof. If it were to be left to outsiders, however learned, to decide on the bonafides of every such declaration, God knows how many good and pious Muslims might have been thrown out of the fold of Islam by unscrupulous elements and Islam would never have spread so rapidly to the four corners of the earth. A Muslim is a Muslim, whether he is sincere or insincere, pious or sinful; it is for Allah to decide on the Day of Judgement.

Imam Abu Hanifa: I agree with my learned colleague, Imam Ghazali. I was once accused by the traditionist, Uthman Batti, that even when a believer went astray I condoned all his lapses; I had explained my position to him in a letter. I would like to quote from it; it is rather long but is relevant to the issue before us:

"Allow me to remind you that before the Apostle of Allah

was assigned his mission, the people were polytheists. He preached to them that there is only one God and asked them to believe in his message. The life and property of anyone who gave up polytheism and adopted Islam became sacred. Then duties were enjoined on those who had embraced the faith. The performance of these duties was termed 'amal' (action). It is this that God refers to when he says: 'Those who had faith and performed good deeds; and those who believed in God and acted virtuously.' There are several *ayats* (verses) of the same kind from which it is clear that the absence of action does not nullify faith, but the absence of affirmation and belief does. That affirmation and action are two separate things, is also evident from the fact that, while in the matter of affirmation all Muslims are equal, they are graded from the point of view of action; for so far as religion and belief are concerned, they are uniform for all Muslims.

"God Himself has said: 'I have prescribed the same religion for you as I charged Noah with. What I revealed to you and what I charged Abraham, Moses and Jesus with was to preserve the religion and not to become divided on it. You should know that guidance.in faith and guidance in work are two different things. You can give the title of *mu'min* even to a person who is unaware of duties: such a person may be ignorant so far as duties are concerned, but he is all the same a believer in respect of affirmation. God Himself has made these distinctions in the Qur'an. Would you equate a person who refuses to acknowledge God and His Apostle with one who, though a believer, is ignorant of practical duties?

"Where the duties are specified in the Qur'an it is said, 'God has stated this so that you do not go astray,' and in another place, 'If one goes astray, let another remind him'. Again, Moses is reported as saying, 'When I did not do that, I was one of those who strayed'. In addition to these verses there are many which clinched the matter. In fact, the other verses are even clearer. Did the title of *Amir al-Muminin* given to Hadrat Umar and Hadrat Ali signify that they were the *Amirs* of only those who performed their practical duties? Hadrat Ali called the people of Syria, who were at war with him, *mu'mins* (true Muslims). Could there be a greater sin than killing? Would you consider both the killers and the killed to be in the right? If you vindicate one party, namely, Hadrat Ali and his supporters, what would you say about the others? Ponder over this and try to understand it. I assert that all Muslims are *mu'mins* and that none of them becomes an infidel by inaction or *beamal*. He who has faith and also performs his duties is a good *mu'min* and destined for Paradise. He who is devoid of both faith and action is an infidel and destined for Hell. He who has faith but fails to act is nevertheless a Muslim, but a sinful one. It is up to God to punish or forgive him."

"That", concluded Imam Abu Hanifa, "is my position; I am sorry for the long quotation but ...."

Imam Ghazali: No one could have put it better; we are, indeed, grateful to Imam Abu Hanifa.

The other Imams did not speak; they only nodded their approval. Imam Ghazali then declared: "Our unanimous verdict is in favour of our sister-in-faith, Benazir. Whether she practises the tenets of Islam or not, it is for Allah to decide on the Day of Judgement; if she does not, she may be consigned to Hell or Allah in his infinite mercy may forgive her for any good, however small, she may do in this world".

The decision brought a sigh of relief to the gathering; only some of the theologians did not seem happy but none dare stir or protest; such was the awe and respect that the members of the Council inspired in everyone present.

Imam Ghazali, while adjourning the proceedings, announced that the Council would take the next issue the following day. He asked the two opposing counsels how long they proposed to take.

Brohi: A few days, I suppose, since the Hon'ble Council has decided to go into the entire issue of a woman's position in Islam.

Ameer Ali: I agree my reverend Imams. I will try to be brief and to the point but the matter needs to be thoroughly examined and finally resolved.

Imam Ghazali: That settles it then; we shall meet tomorrow and see what best we can do to deal with this issue; we shall attempt to clarify it to the best of our abilities.

Yahya Bakhtiar, intervening, pointed out that "the confusion is more in the minds of the non-Muslims than the Muslims. This is mostly due to the misrepresentation of the Christian missionaries and the western intellectuals. One of them, Dr. Peron has written: 'In Islam, women rarely walk the path of saintliness. It is too difficult for them – at least this is what men think. All brilliance, merit and honour goes to the men. They have turned everything to their own advantages and privilege; they have taken for themselves and monopolized everything – even saintliness and Paradise'."

Imam Abu Hanifa: This is preposterous!

Bakhtiar: I agree my venerable Imam; but they quote some Hadith or the other in support of their contention.

Imam Abu Hanifa: That is why I discarded many Hadith; they have done more harm than good to our religion.

Imam Ghazali: We will try to meet all these objections after we have heard both the sides. We hope that Allah will show us the light. After all, we are all in His hands; as He has reminded us in the Quran:

> It is for Allah
> To show us the right direction
> But there are on the way
> Many devious paths. (16:9)

Let us all pray that we do not get lost in these devious paths.

SECTION
III

Is Woman
Subordinate
to Man?

5

The Respondent's Plea

Third Day

No sooner did the Council begin its proceedings than it heard the arguments about the status of woman in Islam — whether she was, in fact, regarded as inferior to man. Imam Ghazali asked the defense counsel, Ameer Ali, to present his point of view first.

Ameer Ali: May I, my reverend Imams, put my ·case briefly before you? I will present the expert witnesses in support of my contention thereafter.

Imam Ghazali: Please do so.

Ameer Ali : The main question to be considered by this Hon'ble Council is, no doubt, whether a woman can be a ruler in an Islamic state or not. However, the issue is very much linked with the larger question, whether a woman has been made, in all respects, equal or subordinate to man. And the basis for such subordination has been found by the classical jurists in this one Quranic verse:

> "Men are the protectors
> And maintainers of women,
> Because God has given
> The one more (strength)
> Than the other, and because
> They support them
> From their means.
> Therefore the righteous women
> Are devoutly obedient, and guard
> In(the husband's) absence
> What God would have them guard.
> As to those women
> On whose part ye fear

Disloyalty and ill-conduct,
Admonish them (first),
(Next), refuse to share their beds,
(And last) beat them lightly;
But if they return to obedience,
seek not against them
Means (of annoyance):
For God is Most High,
Great (above all)". (4:34)

This verse, I submit, concerns the private and marital relationship between a husband and a wife; it is restricted to a particular sphere and has no general bearing on man-woman relationship as a whole.

I am firmly of the opinion that the Quran grants equality of status to woman with man, except in a few limited spheres wherein she may be subordinate due to biological factors, but then in some other respects, she has superiority over man. On the whole, therefore I submit, that the Holy Book upholds equality of sexes. In fact the laws, which the Prophet promulgated, endowed women with rights which they had never possessed before in the history of mankind. He allowed them privileges, the value of which will be more fully appreciated as time advances. I will deal with specific issues as they arise through the observations of expert witnesses. Let me submit humbly that in everything the Prophet said or did, he upheld 'respect for women' and gave them special consideration. That is why in the early centuries of Islam, woman occupied as exalted a position as man. Aisha, the daughter of the first Caliph, Abu Bakr, who was married to the Prophet, personally conducted the insurrectionary movement against the fourth Caliph, Ali. She commanded her own troops at the famous 'Battle of the Camel'. Fatimah, the daughter of the Prophet, often took part in the discussions regarding the succession to the Caliphate. The Prophet's grand daughter, Zainab, the sister of Imam Husain, shielded her youthful nephew from the arrows of Yazid with indomitable courage. Zubaida, the wife of the Abbasid Caliph, Harun, played a notable part in the affairs of the state. Humaida, the wife of King Faruq,

acted as a regent for her son and trained the latter as one of
the most outstanding juriconsults of his times. Sakina, the
beautiful daughter of Imam Husain, held her own among
the most intellectual circles of Medina. Likewise, Buran,
the wife of the Abbasid Caliph Mamun and Umm-ul Fazl,
Mamun's sister, married to the eighth Imam of the Shias,
and Umm-ul Habib, Mamun's daughter were all more
famous for their scholarship than most men of their time.

In the fifth century after the death of the Prophet, Sheika
Shuhda, popularly known as *Fakhrun Nisa* or "the glory of
women" lectured to vast male audiences on religion, literature and the arts. In fact she occupies in the annals of Islam,
a position of equality with the most respected Ulama. Even
on the battle-front, the name of Zat ul-Hemma shines like a
star. The list is illustrative; I have mentioned some of these
names to show that in early Islam, woman had the same
opportunities of growth and development as man. It was
only later that she was confined to the *harem*, forced to wear
the veil which was borrowed from Sassanid Iran, and made
to feel inferior to man. And in bringing about this situation,
the classical jurists misinterpreted certain Quranic verses
and the sayings and the traditions of the Prophet. These
pertain mainly to (1) marriage; (2) divorce; (3) inheritance
and (4) evidence. There are some other matters which may
also need clarification.

My first witness is Allama Abdullah Yusuf Ali, a noted
scholar, whose translation and commentary of the Quran
into English has received universal recognition.

Ameer Ali: Allama Yusuf Ali, does the Quran treat man
and woman as equal?

Yusuf Ali: I have no doubt in my mind about it. In *Surah
Nisa* or the chapter on women, Allah has made this abun-
dantly clear. May I refresh your memory my reverend
Imams.

Imam Malik: You may.

Yusuf Ali: O, mankind!
   Your guardian-Lord,
   Who created you
   From a single Person,
   Created, of like nature,

His mate, and from them twain
Scattered (like seeds)
Countless men and women:—
Reverence God through Whom
Ye demand your mutual (rights),
And (reverence) the wombs
(That bore you): for God _
Ever watches over you. (4:1)

Ameer Ali: Will you please explain its significance?

Yusuf Ali: I believe that sex is among the most wonderful mysteries of nature. The unregenerate male, as a result of his pride in his own physical strength, is likely to forget the all-important part which the female plays in his very existence, and in all the social relationships that arise in our collective human lives. The mother that bore us must ever have our reverence. The wife, through whom we enter parentage, must have our respect. Sex which governs so much of our physical life and has so much influence on our emotional and higher nature deserves not our fear, or our contempt, or our amused indulgence, but our reverence in the highest sense of the term.

Ameer Ali: How does the equality between sexes reconcile with the permission in the Quran for man to marry four wives while woman cannot marry more than one husband?

Yusuf Ali: Before the Quran was revealed, man could marry any number of wives; not four but hundreds; Khusrow Parviz, the Emperor of Iran, had three thousand wives; every religion allowed it. The Quran restricted the number to four, provided the husband can treat them with perfect equality in material things as well as in affection and other immaterial things. As this condition is most difficult to fulfill, I understand the recommendation to be for monogamy.

Brohi, on cross-examination of the witness, conceded the point made by the witness that the Shariah favoured monogamy rather than polygamy, but asked whether under certain circumstances it might not be better to practise polygamy rather than have permissive sexual relationship.

Yusuf Ali: I agree; in such circumstances polygamy is preferable; but the husband has to take care that he loves all wives equally and treats them equitably.

The next witness which Ameer Ali called was the famous Turkish novelist and freedom fighter, Halide Edib Adiyar (1883-1964), who rose to great prominence during the days of the 'Young Turks' movement. She worked closely with Ataturk and was sentenced to death by the Ottoman Sultan Abdul Hamid. Her lectures, books and novels greatly influenced the younger generation of Muslims not only in Turkey but outside as well. Ameer Ali asked her whether she found the Quranic injunctions oppressive against women.

Halide Edib: Not the Quranic injunctions but certainly their interpretations by the classical jurists. I accept the fact that God has made man the head of the family; he has the responsibility of its maintenance; and, in case he fails in this task Imam Malik has rightly opined that the wife has the right to ask for divorce. Your Honour, may I narrate my own personal experience?

Imam Malik: Yes. Please do.

Halide Edib: After completing my education, my parents married me to Salih Zeki Bey, from whom I had two sons. I was happy. I started writing for the nationalist papers espousing the cause of our liberation from the Ottoman yoke. I advocated the education of women and was, for that reason, almost hounded out of Turkey. I got more and more involved in the freedom struggle. Meanwhile, my husband Salih became attracted to a lady teacher. I was shaken by this development. As a believer in monogamy and in the inviolability of my family, I felt morally bound to leave what I had believed would be my home to the end of my life. But knowing Salih Zeki Bey's passing caprices of the heart, before breaking up the family, I wanted to be absolutely sure that his latest attachment would last. I therefore took my little boys with me and went to Yanina to be with my father with the intention of waiting there for a few months.

On my return, Salih Zeki Bey told me that he had married the lady but to my great surprise he added that polygamy was necessary in some cases and asked me to continue as his first wife. There was a long and painful struggle between us; finally he consented to a divorce, and I left for ever what for nine years had been my home.

Ameer Ali: So you were able to get your divorce under the Shariah.

Halide Edib: I managed to get it but with some difficulty; so have innumerable other women. I don't think Islam comes in the way; it is, I am sorry to say, our Ulama, who have clothed the Quranic injunctions with all kinds of oppressive interpretations.

Cross-examining the witness Brohi asked: "Why are you so harsh on our Ulama? Do you know that most of them have opined that a wife could separate from her husband if he ill-treats her."

Halide Edib: I am sorry; I was not aware of that. I thought that they had given unbridled authority to a husband over his wife.

Brohi: On the contrary, a wife has been allowed to secure divorce from her husband in three ways:

(a) by incorporating such a right in the contract of marriage;

(b) on the ground that the husband had ceased to love her;

(c) if he failed to maintain her.

As a fighter for women's rights, were you not aware of these rights which have been given to women by Islam?

Halide Edib: I am truly enlightened. The general conception is that the husband is allowed to rule like a dictator while the wife has to meekly surrender to him.

Imam Malik: Islam has always suffered at the hands of its so-called zealous champions; it has in fact uplifted women as no other religion ever did before. It liberated woman at a time when she was denied even a soul and was sold like a mere chattel.

Ameer Ali was on his feet again. He said: "My third witness is Sayed Mahmud (1850-1903), one of the greatest judges of undivided India and the illustrious son of the founder of Aligarh Muslim University, Sir Sayyid Ahmed Khan. He is as well versed in Anglo-Saxon jurisprudence as he is in Shariah and his juristic eminence has remained undiminished".

Mr. Justice Mahmud stepped into the witness box.

Ameer Ali: Could you tell me, why does the Quran give only half the share to a female child as against that of the male on the death of a parent? Is it not inequitous? I shall quote the relevant verse: 'God commands you concerning your children. For a male the like of the portion of two females'.

Mahmud: I will not go into the history of inheritance; but let me tell you one thing; before the advent of Islam the female did not inherit at all; it is, in fact, the Quran, which for the first time in history, created female heirs. True, on the death of a parent, a son does inherit double the share of a daughter; but the daughter on marriage also gets a separate share in her husband's assets. Again, she gets *mehr* or dower. She does not suffer from any disability in dealing with her estate; she is the absolute master of all that she holds and possesses. The Islamic law of inheritance, I am proud to say, is based on the democratic principles of equality; it was promulgated at the time when such laws were unheard of in Europe or in any other part of the world. Its greatest beneficiaries have been women.

Brohi did not wish to cross-examine Mr. Justice Mahmud.

Ameer Ali's next witness was Begum Ra'ana Liaquat Ali Khan, the widow of the assassinated first Prime Minister of Pakistan and the founder President of the All-Pakistan Women's Association. She was questioned on the *Quanoon-e-Shahadat*, (Law of Evidence) promulgated by the military government of General Zia-ul-Haq, under which the evidence of two female witnesses was equated to that of one male witness.

Begum Liaquat: It is most unjust; the whole tenor of the Quran is in favour of equality of sexes. In so many verses this has been emphasised. General Zia, in order to appease the orthodox Ulama, twisted the meaning of the verse of *Surah al-Baqara* which refers to a specific financial arrangement, The other female witness is in fact to remind the first if she forgets about it. On the basis of this it would be wrong to reduce the value of the evidence of a woman. It does not conform to the general trend of the Quran, which

gives equal weight to the evidence of man and woman. Had
it not been so, the two distinguished compilers of the
sayings and traditions of the Prophet, Imam Bukhari and
Imam Muslim, who are gracing this Council, would not
have relied on the evidence of Bibi Aisha, who is credi-
ted with hundreds of Hadith; these would have required
corroboration by another female member of the Prophet's
family. Likewise, the Companions, accepted the sole evidence of Naila, the wife of the third Caliph, Usman, as the
proof of her husband's murder; no further corroboration
was asked for.

On cross-examination by Brohi, the Begum reiterated
that according to her, in every respect, Islam gave equality
of opportunity and treatment to men and women; it was
later that men had distorted the verses of the Quran and the
traditions of the Prophet.

Ameer Ali next called Dr. Ali Shariati (1933-1977), who
was a Shia theologian and who at one time had the greatest
impact on young Iranians. He came from a highly religious
family but was educated at Sorbonne in Paris. He rebelled
against the establishment, was jailed for his radical views
and was hailed in the leftist circles as the Iranian Fanon. He
was as critical of the westernised elite as of the orthodox
clergymen who gave wrong interpretations to the Quranic
verses and the sayings of the Prophet and the Imams and
lulled the masses into subservience.

Ameer Ali: In your lectures and writings you point out
that Muslim women suffer the most in the name of religion.
Will you kindly elaborate your point?

Shariati: This has happened because Muslims have failed to reconcile the old and the new woman. An age difference of 15, 20 or 30 years between a mother and her
daughter can create two separate entities, two different
kinds of people related to separate societies, cultures, his-
tories, languages, and attitudes and whose relationship is
only apparent from their birth certificates and who have
nothing in common but their home address. We observe
other manifestations of this historic distance between the
two generations and types when we come across a grazing
flock of sheep on the asphalted roads of Teheran and a

shepherd who milks them in front of his buyer where there is also pasteurised milk available. We see a camel by the side of an automatic Jaguar sports car and they span a distance from the time of Cain and Abel to the age of electronics and moon rockets. Similarly, we see a mother and a daughter, walking side by side, who reflect the same distance...

Ameer Ali: What do you wish to suggest?

Shariati: That old forms will inevitably vanish; the new ones will take their place. But the Ulama are trying to resist this transformation. They are using all kinds of methods to suppress them by rousing the people's passions through wrong preaching, artificial moaning and sneering, and even resorting to slander and to beating and punishing of women by distorting the meaning of some Quranic verses. So, instead of reforming women they have driven them to the other extreme — turning them into painted dolls who shop and spend almost with a vengeance.

Ameer Ali: Do you blame the Ulama for all this?

Shariati: I do. They have wasted the energies of our women instead of using them properly; in the name of religion, morality, intergrity, chastity and feminine virtue, they have paralysed them by don'ts — *don't go here, don't do this, don't read that, don't write, don't ask for this, don't ask for that, don't, don't, don't.*

Ameer Ali : What solution do you offer?

Shariati: I feel Muslims will have to be realistic; they must get out of the theological stranglehold. The modern woman is a changed creature; she is not the tame slave of yester-years however comfortably she might have been looked after; nor is she happy to be a useless ornamental doll. She wants to be as useful, resourceful, and assertive as Fatima, the daughter of our Prophet who was his confidante and the true Companion of Imam Ali, her husband. She is the testimony of her father's leadership, her husband's courage and of the honour and glory of her family and nation.

Brohi cross-examined Dr. Shariati.

Brohi: Are you in favour of women working in factories and offices side by side with men?

Shariati: Why not? Those who want to lead an immoral

life can do so even when confined to the four walls of their homes. It is the strength of character and the moral fibre that one possesses that makes the difference. And mark my words, freedom enhances these while prison only weakens them. There is more decency and nobility in the working class women than the so-called respectable ladies in palaces and sheltered homes. I blame the Ulama for the backwardness of women; but the so-called westernised Muslims are even more to blame. Do you know what the deposed, late Shah of Iran told the reporter Oriana Fallaci in 1973; I will quote it for your benefit, with the Council's permission:

'In man's life women only count if they are beautiful and graceful and know how to be feminine... This Women's Lib. business, for instance: What do these feminists want? Equality? I do not want to sound rude, but you may be equal in the eyes of the law but not — I beg your pardon for saying so — in ability. No! You have never produced a Michaelangelo or a Bach. You have not even produced a good cook. And don't talk of opportunities! You must be joking! Have you lacked the opportunity to give history a great cook? You have produced nothing great, nothing.'

And this man was supposed to be a great progressive ruler; he was, in fact, worse than the worst male chauvinist.

Brohi: Thank you, Dr. Shariati. It is really the westernised Muslims rather than the Ulama who have degraded woman and made her the object of man's sexual desire. How many crimes have not been committed in the name of equality of sexes?

Shariati: I entirely agree.

Ameer Ali was somewhat surprised when Brohi called as his witness, Sir Sayyid Ahmad Khan (1817-1898), the father of Sayed Mahmud who had earlier deposed as the witness for Ameer Ali. He was the foremost Muslim leader of undivided India in the late nineteenth century. He founded a college for imparting English education to the Indian Muslims which later became the famous Aligarh Muslim University. An eminent scholar, he was a rationalist in his approach to religion; his commentary on the Quran is most progressive and anti-orthodoxy.

Brohi: Despite your progressive views in all other matters, why are you against women's emancipation?

Sir Sayyid: I am not against their emancipation, but I believe that their rightful place is in the home, where they should provide comfort to their husbands and the best of training to their children.

Brohi: But if they are not educated, what kind of training will they give to their children?

Sir Sayyid: They should be taught privately — at home.

Brohi: You are against their going out and mixing with men.

Sir Sayyid: I am, I don't accept the western approach in this matter. I support the veil and regard the home as the best place for a woman. Also, I think that the tenor of the Quranic teachings is against women's so-called emancipation as we are witnessing in the West.

Ameer Ali cross-examined Sir Sayyid: I could never understand this dichotomy in your attitude. You have done more than any other leader to westernise our boys; why are you then so hide-bound and orthodox in your views about women?

Sir Sayyid: I fear that they might be corrupted by westernisation; I am not prepared to sacrifice their purity for any material gains.

Ameer Ali: Is it not strange that in one breath you talk of *ijtihad* (independent thinking) and in another breath you subscribe to such an outmoded, worn-out philosophy. Alas, what a blind spot you have in this regard!

Sir Sayyid: You may call it a blind spot but I don't think our society is ready for the kind of transformation among women that the West is going through. It may destroy our culture; it may disrupt our social fabric.

Ameer Ali: You are talking like the orthodox Ulama, or classical jurists whom you have otherwise denounced.

Sir Sayyid: My views have nothing to do with those of the orthodox Ulama, or the classical jurists who stick to the letter of the text without understanding either its historical context or its real meaning. I dont accept that any individual or group, however learned, has the right to settle things for us; they cannot intercede between the Creator and His creatures. Our needs today are absolutely different from those of the people of the West. I don't therefore subscribe to the doctrine of *taqlid* or imitation; nor do I accept the juristic doctrine that the doors of *ijtihad* or independent thinking are closed. I believe that in every age, Muslims must reinterpret the Quran and the traditions of the Prophet to suit their requirements. Applying this test, I say that our women, reared and brought up under different moral environment, cannot fit into the western mould. They will be square pegs in round holes.

Ameer Ali: What a contrast between the father and the son on the same issue!

Sir Sayyid: I suppose you will call it the generation gap.

While closing his evidence, Ameer Ali, submitted to the Council that he might be allowed to explain his position on *hijab* or purdah, in case the counsel for the petitioner brought up the matter.

Brohi: I most certainly will.

Imam Ghazali: In that case, we will also give you the opportunity to put your point of view.

Ameer Ali: I am most grateful, Sir.

Imam Ghazali adjourned the proceeding for the day and said Brohi would present his case on the following day.

6

A Question of Equality

Fourth Day

On the fourth day, the President, Imam Ghazali, called Brohi, the counsel for the petitioners, to proceed with his presentation.

Brohi: The pith and substance of the case for equality between man and woman that my learned friend, Syed Ameer Ali has presented is more on the western than on Islamic lines. I agree with him that the Quran has given greater equality to woman than she had ever been given in the past in any society; but there is a difference between the western and the Islamic approach. While the West has in defiance of the teachings of both Christianity and Judaism, which relegate woman to the lowest level, tried to obliterate the differences between the sexes, Islam gives due recognition to these differences and chalks out separate spheres of activities for the two. In his or her own respective sphere, a man or a woman is, more or less, supreme; but overall the supremacy of man is recognised. I would like to ask, my learned friend, if, despite all the liberation movements that have been unleashed by the so-called female liberators, the supremacy of man in practice has been undermined. No one can fight nature; what Allah has willed through His acts cannot be undone. Islam respects the status of woman; she is an equal partner with man. But her role is different from man; both man and woman are complementary to each other. Those who are trying to make them into rivals will strike at the very root of family which Islam cherishes as a most valuable institution.

My first witness is the founder of that puritanical movement in Arabia known as Wahhabism. He helped King Abdal Aziz ibn Saud to found the kingdom of Saudi Arabia.

His name is Muhammad ibn Abdal Wahhab (1703-1787). He carried forward the fundamentalist interpretation of Islam which was, so ably expounded by my Imam Hanbal.

Imam Ghazali: We will be pleased to hear his views.

Brohi: May I know, ibn Wahhab, whether you subscribe to the view that the Quran treats men and women as equal.

Ibn Wahhab: Yes and no. Allah has created different species for different purposes; in their own spheres, everyone is equal, provided he or she is virtuous. Superiority comes out of virtue and not out of race, sex or progeny. If *A* were to do the work of *B*, there will be no system; nature works systematically, not chaotically. Man creates chaos; Allah, order. That is why He demands that we should follow His commands and there would be peace and harmony in the world. The trouble arises when man tries to tamper with His system or disobeys His orders.

Brohi: What relevance has this to man-woman relationship?

Ibn Wahhab: As much as to any other relationship or functioning. Obey Allah and His Prophet and everything will be all right; disobey and everything will go wrong. The Quran divides man and woman into two; in fact Allah has created them differently. Hence they have to work separately under the divine scheme. Woman is meant for the home and man for the world outside.

Cross-examined by Ameer Ali, ibn Wahhab maintained that the Quranic approach in this regard was clear; but the westernised Muslims had distorted its verses and given wrong interpretations to them.

Brohi then requested the Council to permit him to recall Maududi.

Imam Ghazali: You may do so.

Maududi stepped into the witness-box.

Imam Ghazali: You are already under oath.

Maududi: Yes, my Imam.

Brohi: Maulana, do you believe in the equality of sexes?

Maududi: Yes, I do. Men and women are two equal parts of the human race. Both have a heart, mind, intellect, emotions, desires and needs. In this respect, the claim of equality is totally correct and it is the duty of every virtuous society to allow women to progress but only according to their natural capacity and capability. It must give to women too their social and economic rights and a status of honour in the social order. Also, a sense of self respect. Westernised women have become morally debased; their own children do not respect them. Hence they can never rear them properly.

Brohi: Can you say this about all western mothers?

Maududi: Well, it is a question of their attitude. Islam aims at canalising man's sex energy by moral discipline with a view to building a clean and pious culture; the West, on the other hand, is only interested in material progress by inducing man and woman to participate equally in all the affairs of life. This contradicts the basic objective of Islam which is to establish a social order that separates the activities of man and woman, discourages and controls the free intermingling of the two and curbs all such factors as are likely to upset and jeopardise social discipline.

Brohi: How will free mingling upset social discipline?

Maududi: An intelligent person can easily visualise the result. Islam has deliberately put certain restrictions on the movement of women. They are asked to cover themselves fully except for the hands and the face;they can go out of their homes only for genuine needs. They should not speak to strangers. But the West encourages them to display their physical charms so as to satisfy the sexual lust of men. Wives, sisters and daughters, dressed up and fully made-up, mix with men in a manner and to an extent unimaginable in Islam. They are allowed to move freely on the streets, stroll in the parks, visit hotels, clubs and cinema houses in glamorous attires with their bosoms and shoulders barely covered. I was shocked to see Turkish women, bathing on the beaches, wearing bathing suits, shamelessly displaying their bodies. Has the Quran permitted nudity? Is it in conformity with the teachings of our Prophet?

Brohi: If a woman were to dress sedately and behave 'properly' in public, can she then participate in public affairs.

Maududi: Most certainly not. A woman is meant primarily for the home; we should not degrade her by making her run after social, economic or political pursuits. These are bound to take her away from her home, her husband and her children; the inevitable casualty is the family which is the basis of any civilization. I ask you, why should a woman subject herself to moral and legal curbs if she is economically independent? Why should she not do then as she pleases? Why should she be faithful to her husband and not be free of all moral and social restrictions? And what is then to become of the children? In liberating the woman, are we not killing the mother? Man cannot replace her; she is the pivot round whom human life revolves.

Ameer Ali rises to cross-examine Maududi.

Ameer Ali: You have made out a strong case for the segregation of woman; but are you aware that as a result of it she has been the victim of man's sexual greed, physical oppression and economic repression?

Maududi: Who is responsible for it? Not Islam but the defiance of its tenets by man. If man had followed the injunctions of the Quran and the traditions of the Prophet, he would have treated the woman as a queen. The Prophet has said, 'He is the best of my followers who treats his woman the best'.

Ameer Ali: But human nature being what it is, this has not happened.

Maududi: Islam came to change the barbaric nature of man; if we follow it sincerely, there will be no oppression or repression.

The next witness Brohi called was Fareed Wajdi, the noted scholar from Al-Azhar, who had challenged Qasim Amin; he wrote a book called "*The Muslim Woman*" in reply to the former's "*The Modern Woman*". Their encounters have become a part of Islamic literature.

Brohi: Why are you such a zealous advocate of *hijab* or purdah for woman?

Wajdi: Because our culture, which is entirely different from that of the West, so requires; our women are our treasures; we don't want them to be wasted in offices and factories; they are the adornments of our homes, the guardians of our children, the solace and comfort of the husbands. For almost two hundred years we have mixed with the Europeans, aped their way of life; but our women wear the *hijab* even today. They are not prepared to discard it because it protects them against the villainy and rapaciousness of men. The day Muslim women give up their veil, Islam will be destroyed.

While getting up to cross-examine Wajdi, Ameer Ali commented: They are giving it up now and no one can stop them from doing so any more.

Then, turning to Wajdi he asked: Your book was a reply to Qasim Amin's *al-Maratul Jadida* or "The Modern Woman". In his book, Amin has pointed out that the veil was an obstacle to the development of the woman; it deprives her of earning her livelihood; it makes her economically dependent on the man; it ostracises her socially; it makes her a chattel, with the result that she becomes incapable of being a good mother to her children. Don't you agree that this has been the fate of most Muslim women, irrespective of the treatment that our religion enjoins upon our men to give to their women?

Wajdi: Even if that were true, it is because we are not faithful to our creed. This applies not only to man-woman relationship but to all other spheres of human activity. Man is weak, prone to all kinds of temptations but even the worst of men want their mothers, sisters, daughters and wives to have the best in the world. He struggles to keep a happy home; that is a part of his true nature. Even the West has acknowledged that behind every successful man there is always a woman; Islam has tried to give her the highest and the noblest place in the world.

Ameer Ali: But why not educate her fully and make her an equal and useful partner of her husband instead of shutting her out from the rest of the world? The women during the Prophet's time participated in so many activities including joining the men on the battlefield.

Wajdi: I agree; they did but where is that moral and social environment? Today they are surrounded by evil all around them; it is best that they are guarded from the viles, corruption and degradation of modern society.

Brohi called his next witness, the Egyptian scholar, Muhammad Qutb, who was one of the ideologues of the

Muslim Brotherhood, founded by Hasan al-Banna, a school teacher in Cairo. The Brotherhood stood for Islamic fundamentalism and the return of the Muslims to the purity and piety of early Islam. Banna did not leave much written material behind; but after his death, Sayyid Qutb and his brother Muhammad Qutb propagated his mission and through their numerous books, written in an incisive and effective style, carried the message forward. They clashed with Nasser and his Free Officers and were in consequence, imprisoned and even tortured. Sayyid Qutb was charged with conspiracy to murder Nasser and hanged. Mohammed Qutb continued the missionary work which his brother had undertaken with unbounded devotion and zeal.

Brohi: In your book: *Man between Islam and Materialism*, you have dealt at length with the problem of equality of sexes.

Qutb: Yes, I have. However I don't subscribe to equality; I say men and women are different. I have tried to explain the Islamic point of view as best as I could. I believe that Islam stands for the protection of women much more solidly than the West which has cast a spell on many of our so-called modern and secular Muslims. They want to bring equality between two species of human beings, who are so very different in their constitution and disposition and who are equipped by nature to perform entirely different functions. They are complementary to each other; but they can never be equal. To my mind, motherhood is the main function of a woman; it is the soul of the family, which is the basis of civilization.

Brohi: Do you mean to say that the function of one cannot be performed by the other?

Qutb: No, I don't mean that. I concede that the two sexes cannot be totally compartmentalized and that a water-tight division may not be possible. But what is happening in the West today where women are supposed to have gained all the rights? There is utter confusion and chaos. I admit that there have been women who have proved to be capable of ruling, of dispensing justice and even of lifting heavy burdens and fighting in wars; similarly, there have been men who have been good cooks and excellent housekeepers, but they are the exceptions. They do not prove what the misguided Westerners and their slavish imitators in the East are trying to prove: that man can do whatever woman can and woman can do whatever man can. A woman, wherever and in whatever position she may be, wants a home, a companion and caretaker in her husband, a family of her own and above all, children. Islam recognises this natural urge and its tenets are in conformity with it.

Brohi: Why should she then not be the head of the family and why should she inherit merely half the assets of her parents as compared to her brother?

Qutb: I shall deal with the question of the head of the family first. Why should the man be that and not the woman? Because, man is better equipped for this task. He is more rational, less emotional; the stronger the man, the more he is admired by the woman; while the stronger the woman, the less she is liked by the man. Who can deny that a physically well-built man is more attractive to a woman than a weakling. Or that a delicate damsel rouses much greater feeling of affection in a man than a huge, hefty woman.

This does not however mean that man should be a dictator and lord over the woman or over his house arbitrarily, for leadership entails obligations and duties which can be discharged only through mutual consultation and cooperation. Islam insists that love, mutual understanding and perpetual sympathy rather than conflict and competition should form the basis of family life. Says the Holy Quran: "Consort with them in kindness," (4:19), and the Holy Prophet said: "Best amongst you is he who is good to his wife." The gauge thus laid down by the Holy Prophet to judge a man is his behaviour towards his wife. And a very sound standard it is, for no man can ill-treat his wife unless he is spiritually diseased and absolutely lost to virtue or is morally handicapped.

Brohi: Why does the Quran then allow the husband to beat his wife?

Qutb: You must understand the context in which this is mentioned; in case a wife refuses to have sex with him what should the husband do? Should he seek to establish illicit relations with other women? No society can approve of such a course, nor can the wife herself agree that her husband should go to another woman. So long as they live together as husband and wife, the wife must, according to Islamic law, comply with the wish of her husband and satisfy his sexual needs. It does not necessarily imply an arbitrary authority or compulsion. It is meant to prevent the husband from being driven to pursue a course of moral perversion or entering into another marriage contract, which would be all the more painful for the wife to bear. The law however does not insist on the continuance of relations wherein the wife feels repulsion for her husband. They may in such a case separate.

Brohi: What about the satisfaction of a woman's sexual urge? Can she demand it from an unwilling husband?

Qutb: The Shariah is clear on this point. The man cannot disregard her needs either. The very law that lays the wife under an obligation to comply with the wish of her husband also ensures that she too should have equal rights. It prescribes that the husband must also fulfil his marital duties if and when his wife should so desire. If the husband is unable to satisfy her, their marriage may dissolve. Thus we see that in Islamic law, both parties have got their duties as well as their rights. The wife has the same rights as the husband while he has the same duties and obligations as she has.

Brohi: But she cannot divorce him as the husband can, if the two cannot get along!

Qutb: This is another canard spread against Islam by the West. The wife has three ways in which to seek separation from her husband.

(a) She can secure the right to divorce from her husband (at the time of entering into the marriage contract with him). The Islamic law explicitly allows it although few women ever exercise it. The right is however there which the woman can exercise if she so desires.

(b) She can demand a divorce from her husband on the plea that she does not like him and can no longer live with him. I have heard that some courts do not enforce this principle and do not decree a woman's separation from her husband when she is the one seeking it although the principle is clearly laid down and supported by the personal example of the Holy Prophet and is thus a part of the Islamic law. The only condition for the woman in such a case is that she should give back to her husband the dowry she received from him — a perfectly just condition. The husband too in the event of divorcing his wife is obliged to forgo in her favour all that he might have given her. Thus, in order to free themselves, both man and woman have to bear material loss in equal manner.

(c) The third course open to the wife is to secure a divorce by surrendering her dower, provided she is able to convince the court that her husband has ill-treated her or has failed to give her the sustenance allowance agreed upon by both of them and furnish the necessary proofs thereof. The court shall dissolve the marriage contract if it is convinced of the legitimacy of her claims.

These are the safeguards which a woman may claim. They perfectly balance the authority that man enjoys over her.

Brohi: What about polygamy? How can it be justified?

Qutb: Why do women not ask for four husbands if they really want equality? No. They would never do so because that would make them miserable. Islam does not sanction polygamy as a rule; it is an emergency law. The Quran gives conditional approval; it says:

"Marry of the women, who seem good to you, two or three or four; and if ye fear that ye cannot do justice (to so many) then one (only)." (4 : 3).

As pointed out in this verse, what is required of men is to do justice to all his wives which is the most difficult to achieve; the injunction hence virtually implies that men should contract with one wife only. Islamic law in normal life favours monogamy rather than polygamy. But there are certain circumstances under which monogamy becomes an unjust rather than a just institution. In such extraordinary circumstances, Islamic law leaves the door open to polygamy, for although complete justice is impossible to attain, the disadvantages resulting therefrom are far less serious than those flowing from monogamy in emergencies.

Brohi: Then why is the Muslim woman so unhappy with her lot?

Qutb: Because she is ignorant of what Islam offers her. For instance: She demands an equal status with man. But Islam has already given this to her, in theory as well as in practice before law.

She wants economic independence and the right to participate in social life directly. Well, Islam was the first religion that gave her this right.

She wants to be educated? Islam not only recognizes the need but makes the knowledge obligatory on her.

She wants that she should not be given in marriage without her permission. Islam has given her this right as well as the right to arrange her own marriage.

Does she demand that she should be treated kindly and fairly while performing her functions within the house? And that she should have the right to ask for a separation from her husband if he should fail to treat her in a just and fair manner? Islam does give her all these rights and makes it incumbent upon a man to safeguard them.

Finally, if she wants the right to go and work outside, Islam recognizes this right too.

Brohi: Now coming to the question of inheritance, the Quranic formula is: "To the male the equivalent of the portion of two females". How do you justify it?

Qutb: It is quite natural because the Quran puts the responsibility of looking after the family on the man. The woman is under no obligation to spend money on anyone but her own person except ofcourse when she becomes the head of the family but such a situation is very rare. In an Islamic society, as long as a woman has a male relation howsoever distant she need not take upon herself the support of her family. Can such an arrangement be termed as injustice towards woman, as the votaries of feminism claim? Leaving aside these vain postulations and prejudiced claims, the problem is just one of simple reckoning: on the whole woman gets one third of the inherited property to spend on her person, whereas man is given two thirds of it to discharge his financial obligations in the first place, towards his wife (that is the woman), and secondly towards

his family and children. As such, speaking in terms of
simple mathematics, to whom does the larger portion go?
There may be certain men who are wont to spend all their
money on themselves and are disinclined to marry or beget
a family, but such cases are uncommon. Normally it is the
man who shoulders the financial burdens of his family,
including that of the woman, his wife, not as an act of grace
but as a moral obligation. If a woman possesses property of
her own, her husband cannot take it away from her without
her consent; he would, even then have to bear her financial
burden, as if she had nothing in her possession to support
herself with. And if he should refuse her this allowance or
should he be miserly in proportion to his income, she can
lodge a complaint against him in the court and force him to
give her the sustenance allowance or get free from him.
There is as such, no justification to say that in inheritance
woman receives a share less than that of man. In view of his
obligations, it is but natural that a man should get double the
share of a woman.

Brohi: This is about inheritance. What about her earnings?

Qutb: So far as her earnings are concerned there is no
difference between man and woman; neither in wages for
work, nor in the profit gained in trade, nor in revenues
from land etc.; for, in these matters Islam follows another
law, the law treating man and woman on a perfectly equal
footing with regard to their labours and the wages thereof.

Ameer Ali cross-examined Qutb: "I agree with most of
your interpretations; but in reality, man has ill-treated woman and no *alim* or mullah has protected her against it.
How do you explain this dichotomy between the tenets and
the attitude of our theologians who have always leaned in
favour of man?"

Qutb: You are right; we have failed to protect the rights
of our women. The woman in Islamic countries is generally
backward, she lives a life similar to that of animals; her
whole existence is but another name for mean earthly desires; she suffers privations more than she ever tastes of
happiness; she is made to surrender more than she is given;
she seldom rises above the level of a purely impulsive

existence. This is also true, but may we ask: who is responsible for this state of affairs? Does Islam or its teachings
have anything to do with it?

Ameer Ali: Who is responsible?

Qutb: The fact is that the miserable plight of the Muslim
woman is the result of the economic, social, political and
psychological conditions prevailing in the Muslim world
today. We must take note of these if we really want to
reform our social life and know as to where these evils
spring from. At the root of the present miserable plight of
our women lies the wretched prevalent poverty. It is the
social injustice which makes a group of people live in lu-
xury and profusion whereas their fellow beings do not have
enough to feed or clothe themselves properly. To make
matters worse, there is political repression which splits a
people into the ruler and the ruled, the former enjoying all
privileges without the attendant obligations, and the latter
labouring under heavy burdens with no rights or compen-
sations in return. The dark clouds of oppression that over-
cast the heavens above are the result of these very social
factors. It is these circumstances that are in effect responsible for the present humiliation and persecution of Muslim
woman.

Ameer Ali: Does that not apply equally to men and
women?

Qutb: It does, but a woman suffers more, she is so constituted. She craves for an amicable relationship of love and
mutual respect between her and her companion. But how
can love and respect find expression in the suffocating
atmosphere of bleak poverty and social repression? So the
man treats the woman roughly and persecutes her as a
reaction to the harsh treatment and persecution that he
himself suffers at the hands of the people around him. He
feels disgraced, his pride is wounded. He meets nothing
but humiliation in social life. He cannot avenge himself
against these antagonistic forces; so he comes home and
gives vent to his anger against his wife. It is this accursed
poverty that exhausts man totally incapacitating him and
leaving him devoid of love, sympathy or forebearance towards those among whom he lives. And strange as it may

sound, it is that very wretched poverty that makes a woman put up patiently with tyranny, cruelty and the rough
treatment from her husband for she knows that life without
a bread-winner would be even worse. She dare not claim
her legal rights fearing that her husband might divorce her.
And what would she do if he divorced her? Who will
support her? Thus, she needs protection but in the Islamic
way not the western way.

Ameer Ali: Will the Islamic way that you prescribe remove poverty and social disgrace?'

Qutb: Most assuredly; it will also reduce man's greed and
by inculcating mutual co-operation and respect for one
another it will eliminate the roots of inequality of income
and wealth, thus bringing in an era of peace and prosperity
for all — as was witnessed in early Islam.

Ameer Ali sought the permission of the Council to examine three Muslim women who had discarded the veil,
mixed freely with men of their times, and had made a mark
for themselves. The first was Walladah bint al-Mustakfi,
(1001-1080), the daughter of the Arab ruler who lived in the
Moorish Kingdom of Cordova in Spain; she was beautiful,
full of grace and charm.She was interested in poetry, not
men. On the fall of her father's kingdom when she was
about thirty, Walladah discarded the veil, wrote some of
the great poems in Arabic and opened her house to men of
arts and letters; many of them fell in love with her, but she
was lost in her poetry and remained unmarried.

Ameer Ali: Why did you discard the veil?

Walladah: It is of no use; it cannot guard the chastity of a
woman; it is the mind, which guards it and not the body.

Ameer Ali: Ibn Khaqan, the historian, has said that you
'bewitched the hearts and minds of those around you, that
your presence encouraged the old to behave like the
young'.

Walladah: But both the old and the young knew that I
was like the deer of Mecca, whose hunting was forbidden.

Ameer Ali: Did you not encourage the poet Ibn Zaydun?

Walladah: I liked him but all he was interested in was my
flesh; when I did not respond, he enticed my black maid.
Oh, they are all the same — these men! I chided Ibn Zaydun

in one of my poems. He was furious and described me, in one of his poems, "like water, difficult to hold in hand". So I was. Despite giving up my veil, I did not surrender my chastity to any man. No man dared misbehave with me.

Cross-examining, Brohi asked her whether she was not the subject of much controversy and even gossip.

Walladah: Yes; but when have men ever left women alone, whether with the veil or without it; it is men who need the veil, not women.

The second lady, whom Ameer Ali summoned as a witness, was the Algerian freedom fighter and journalist, Fadela M'rabet. She comes of an orthodox religious family, many of her forbears have been Ulama. She discarded the veil and moved freely; she specialised in mass communication. A well-known radio and T.V. personality, she has written several books championing the cause of Muslim women's emancipation.

Ameer Ali: Though you come from a family of well-known theologians, you have condemned the orthodox attitude to women in your writing. What is the cause for this revolt?

M'rabet: The degradation of women. May I elaborate my reverend Imams?

Imam Ghazali: Yes. You may.

M'rabet: I hope I will be forgiven if I speak frankly.

Imam Ghazali: You may speak freely.

M'rabet: Our Ulama insist that the Quran has assigned an inferior status to a woman; if that is so, why do they say then that Islam has elevated the status of women. They say we are physically weak; but so what? Are we not mentally their equal? Again and again, we are told that women are meant for men (16:74 and 30:20), never is it said that men are also meant for women. We are the source of their pleasure, the warrior's repose. We are to bear them children (30:20) and to be like their field, where they could plough and sow as they liked (2:223). Men's dominance over women has been explicitly mentioned (2:288), but there is no verse about women. The explanation given is that men spend their wealth on them. (4:38). Hence they have even been given the right to beat them (women)

(Ibid). Man can marry four wives; but a woman is allowed only one husband (4:3). He can have sex with many women, wives and concubines; but a woman is deprived of even the slightest latitude. (60: 29,30,33 and 48). He can dress as he likes but she must live and move as if in a tent. Man can dispose of his goods as he wants, but a woman cannot, except a third, without his permission. He can divorce her, without a cause, she has to suffer him for the rest of her life. Even when she is allowed to inherit, it is only half the share of the male heir. Is this equality, I ask? I concede that the rights which the Prophet gave to women were far in advance of the times he lived in; but should we not judge the Quranic verses in the spirit of his reforms instead of by merely sticking to the letter of the texts?

Brohi, on cross-examination, asked her only one question: "Have you studied the Quran properly and understood the background and meaning of these verses?"

M'rabet: I am no scholar; I will be happy to be enlightened on the proper meaning of the Quranic verses.

Brohi: I am sure the Council will do it. Then you will realise how wrong you have been in your approach. No religion upholds the equality of man and woman as Islam does; the verses you have quoted have to be understood in their proper context.

Ameer Ali called the last witness Jehan Sadat, the widow of the assassinated President, Anwar Sadat of Egypt. A lady of distinction, beautiful, intelligent and courageous, she has suffered much since the tragic death of her husband. She has been a fighter for women's rights and had campaigned vigorously for reforms in the personal laws for women, especially in marriage and divorce and succeeded in getting the Egyptian women a better deal.

Ameer Ali: What was the reaction of your husband, the President, his colleagues and other dignitaries to your demand for better treatment of women?

Jehan Sadat: My husband was, at first, rather chary; his colleagues were also unhelpful. They were afraid that the fundamentalists would raise a hue and cry if women were given more rights. But gradually Anwar was convinced that women needed greater protection from men. He ap-

pointed, therefore, a committee to examine the question
and nominated as its members among others, three of the
highest religious authorities in the country — Muhammad
Abdul Rahman Bisar, Shaikhul Azhar, Shaikh Muhammad
Abdal Muneem al-Nimr — the Minister for Religious En-
dowments — and Shaikh Gad al-Haq, the Grand Mufti of
Egypt. The committee, after careful scrutiny of the Quranic
texts, the Hadith and the various *fatwas* recommended a
package of mild reforms:

A judicial court to appoint arbiters in case of dispute
between a husband and wife, preferably of relatives with a
view to reconcile differences and prevent a divorce; the
husband to inform promptly his wife, in case he had divorced her; also to inform the first wife, in case he has decided
to take another wife, the first wife to have the right to seek a
divorce within twelve months; the divorced mother to
have the right to retain custody of the children at least until
her sons reach ten years of age and her daughters twelve, or
longer, if the court found it beneficial to the children; the
divorced women in certain cases to have the right to collect
not only alimony from their ex-husbands but also a lump
sum whose amount increases in proportion to the length of
their marriage period; and lastly the right of the divorced
mother to retain the family home. However, as soon as
these reforms were published, there were protests from the
fundamentalists. One of their most vocal leaders, railed
against these reforms every week after Friday prayers and
condemned them as 'Jehan's Laws' saying:

' These laws she wants will turn men into women and
women into men. They will cause the break-down of the
Egyptian family structure and move hundreds to godless-
ness! These laws are against the Shariah. By the end of the
year there were articles for and against the reforms in
almost every Arab newspaper and periodical; the debates
grew hotter, the pressure more intense. What hurt was the
campaign by the fundamentalists against women's character. They distorted the Quranic texts and the Hadith to
show how we are physically weak and emotionally unstable. One Shaikh said that if a woman was told that her
husband had taken other wives, she would get excited and

demand a divorce without thinking or trying to reconcile. From every pulpit, the fundamentalists screamed that 'a woman has to stay at home to cook, to wash, to clean, to care for the children.' They demeaned the image of man.

Ameer Ali: What was the reaction of your husband?

Jehan Sadat: He was somewhat taken aback by the fury that the fundamentalists had unleashed; what disturbed him was the rioting that broke out. Here in the Al-Azhar area, hundreds of male students shouted against the reforms, marching around the University courtyard in the white robes and skullcaps of the devout. They bellowed: "We want *one, two, three, four* wives." Cartoons were posted on the bulletin boards of the University, showing me as a man in a military uniform. What shocked me was the attitude of even the so-called progressive, westernised Muslims. At almost every social function I attended, the husbands took me aside to whisper vehemently that though they wholeheartedly supported most of these reforms they were opposed to only one: the family home to be given to the divorced wife. In Cairo especially it has never been easy to find a place to live in; they were, therefore, not ready to surrender it. 'Where would we live?' they asked, 'on the street', I replied. 'As a man you can live anywhere; but don't throw your wife on the street. You know what will happen'. They had no answer. My husband could not resist our demand any longer; on June 20, 1979 he issued the first of two Presidential decrees about women, reserving 30 seats for women in Parliament; and 20 per cent on provincial councils. His second decree was much closer to my heart; it concerned the reforms in marriage and divorce laws, as recommended by the committee. It was, indeed, a very bold step, considering it took place at the time when the fundamentalists, under the leadership of Ayotullah Khomeini, had toppled the Shah's regime in Iran.

Brohi, while cross-examining, sympathised with Jehan Sadat for the tragedy she suffered, but asked her whether these reforms were not abrogated by the Egyptian Parliament after the death of her husband.

Jehan Sadat: Not at all. In 1985, the Egyptian Supreme Court struck down the amendments we had succeeded in introducing in the Personal Laws. However, within a few months, the Parliament ratified these and declared them consistent with the Shariah. As a result, the divorce rate has fallen considerably, almost by 30 per cent, every year. May be husbands are reluctant to give up the family home.

Brohi: So it is more the fear of losing the family home rather than the wife, which is preventing divorces.

Jehan Sadat: You should know better.

Brohi requested the President of the Council to allow him to produce one lady witness against the three weighty ones which Ameer Ali put in the witness box.

Ghazali: There seems to be a race between the two sides. Will there be one or more?

Brohi: Only one more, my venerable Imam. My learned friend Ameer Ali has already won the race, I can't compete with him. I believe in quality rather than quantity. However, since he has put forth so many women I don't like the impression to go round that women are with him. On the contrary most women support our viewpoint and are against all this talk of emancipation and liberation.

Ameer Ali: On what basis is my learned friend making his claim? Has there been a referendum?

Brohi: No, but I am ready for one.

Ghazali: Ours is not an election tribunal; what is the purpose of this encounter?

Brohi: My respectful Imam, may I present before you a remarkable woman, who has rendered yoeman service to Islam? She is a westerner, a Jewish convert to Islam. Her name is Maryam Jameelah. She hails from New York and was educated in some of the best American schools; she is a renowned intellectual. She is deeply interested in religion, philosophy, history, sociology and such related subjects. Islam began to attract her since she was very young; it so fascinated her that she got converted to our faith and came under the wings of Maulana Maududi's Jamaat-i-Islami. In 1962, she migrated to Pakistan and married one Yusuf Khan, who had already a wife. She became a mother of four children and found no difficulty in living under the same roof with her co-wife and the latter's children. She has also taken to the veil and written numerous books praising the rituals and traditions of Islam.

Maryam Jameelah stepped into the witness-box. She was draped from head to toe in a white chaddar, a thin veil covered her face. In a soft but clear voice she took the oath on the Quran.

Brohi: Why are you such an ardent advocate of *hijab* or the veil?

Jameelah: Because I know too well, the crimes that are committed by women who go about openly and mix with men without any let or hindrance. I have seen unveiled girls parading in uniform, marching through the streets of Washington, waving banners and shouting political slogans. I have seen women exhibiting themselves in beauty contests in semi-nude attires. I have seen women neglecting their homes, spending most of their time out of doors campaigning in elections. I have seen them sweat in factories. I have seen them work as secretaries and executives falling a prey to man's carnal desires. Islam cannot tolerate such perversion of social and cultural values. *Hijab* is their best protector; it may keep them away from the glamour of public life but it is far better for them to do so than to become a victim of man's lust.

Brohi: What about polygamy? You also support it.

Jameelah: I know from personal experience how well it works if one can free oneself from petty jealousies. There is nothing like sharing the bed of one's husband with another woman. It is far better than the husband going out secretly to prostitutes and cheating on his wife. Polygamy helps to check immorality and propensities of men. It also saves innocent women from being deserted. Those, who demand a ban on polygamy are consciously or unconsciously encouraging men to throw the first wife to the wolves; if they are honest they should also demand a ban on divorce. That is the Christian teaching; but it has proved disastrous.

Brohi: Are you against the feminist movement for equality with men?

Jameelah: Well, the feminist movement is not a modern phenomenon; it has its roots in ancient times. In his book: *Republic,* Plato called for the abolition of the family; in the classical Greek comedy, *Lyistrata* the separate functions of

men and women are ridiculed. Coming to the nineteenth
century, Henrick Ibsen, in his play, *A Doll's House* has
preached the same; the Victorian philosopher, John Stuart
Mill mouthed the same views, so did Marx's friend, the
German socialist theoretician, Federich Engels. Engels in
his essay, *The Subjugation of Women*, called marriage a
'dreary mutation of slavery'. The modern feminists have
drawn their inspiration from them; their leaders have agita-
ted for the fulfillment of these ideas and have come to the
conclusion that without political power their emancipation
and liberation was not possible. Hence in the name of
human rights they are asking for more and more political
power. One has only to look at the American Seneca Falls
Convention of 1848. What did it demand? Complete control
of women on their property and earning, the right to divorce their husbands, guardianship over the children and
an end to sexual discrimination in employment along with
the right to receive equal pay with men for the same work.
And how does one go about achieving these ends? Female
franchise? Political power? As their movement grew, they
concentrated on one thing; women's suffrage, until every
country, one by one, had to concede it. They are more
interested in politics than their homes, their families, their
children. Soon we shall have to nationalise our children —
they would have no mothers to care for them. Some state
agency will have to undertake the responsibility.

Brohi: Do these feminists really want the abolition of the
family?

Jameelah: Have you any doubt about it? Let me remind
you of what happened at the feminists' demonstration in
New York on August 26, 1970; it was the largest demonstration of its kind in the world. Thousands of women (mostly
young), marched down Fifth Avenue in New York carrying
placards, which read: **Housewives are unpaid slaves; The
state must pay for housework; Oppressed women — don't
cook dinner; Starve your husband tonight; End human
sacrifice; Don't get married. Have sex with any man you
like; Legalise abortion; Dependency is not a healthy state
of being.** They have declared war on men; they don't want
equality: they want man's subjugation. Judith Hole and

Ellen Levine in their book: *The Rebirth of Feminism* have categorically declared: 'We want to be full people, crippled neither by law nor custom nor chained minds. If there is no room for that in nature then nature must be changed'.

Brohi: That sounds frightening. How can Islam ever be reconciled to it?

Jameelah: Oh! It is even worse. Some of the Feminist leaders openly advocate sex between women — lesbianism — as the only road to political power, and for ending the oppression of men.

Ameer Ali in his cross-examination, asked Jameelah, whether she had not damned the entire womankind by her observations when she narrated the demands of the few among them. Surely the West has not abandoned the family?

Jameelah: True, it is still there, but it is rapidly disintegrating. Muslims have to ward off the West's evil influence which is becoming increasingly materialistic. And materialism has to be fought single-mindedly or else it will overtake us all. It is always the few who create the mischief, but the consequences of it have to be suffered by society as a whole.

Imam Ghazali looked at the clock and adjourned the proceedings announcing that they would meet the next morning, when they would pronounce their verdict on the question of the status of woman in Islam.

7

The General Decision

Fifth Day

The Council met in the midst of anxious expectations. Would it declare woman subordinate to man? If so, there would be no further discussion. The main contention of the petitioners that a woman cannot be a ruler would then be upheld. The President of the Council took the rostrum and began to pronounce the verdict:

"It is strange that after almost 1,400 years there are divergent views about the real status of woman in Islam. We, on this Council, are unanimous that neither the Quran nor the Prophet has shown anything but the highest respect and regard for her. The first follower of the Prophet was a woman — his wife Khadija; when he was visibly shaken on receiving the divine message, it was she who restored and strengthened his faith. For twenty-five years she was his constant companion; without her help he would not have succeeded in his mission. He stopped female infanticide; restricted polygamy; frowned upon divorce; and gave women a status, which they had never enjoyed anywhere in the world. Instead of complaining why he did not do this and that we must wonder how he was able to achieve so much in so short a time. Moreover, the Quran gave women so much without their asking; there was no feminist movement then. And all this was given to them in the seventh century whereas in Europe, which is spearheading the feminist movement today, women were condemned as evil and more than a million were burnt alive as witches until as late as the eighteenth century.

There is a fierce race going on now for equality between man and woman; but what has been Islam's contribution?

I have already referred in my previous judgement to the

Quranic verse (4:11), wherein Allah calls upon mankind to
    Reverence God, through whom
    Ye demand your mutual rights
    And (reference) the wombs
    (That bore you):
Mark you, the reverence to woman (the womb that bore
you) follows the reverence to God. At what heights and
majesty – women have been placed. Moreover, all believers, men and women, have been put on a part (49.10).
Again, according to a Hadith, as recorded by my Imam
Muslim, the Prophet received the commitment oath from
both men and women.

"In surah Baqara (2) there are verses, which relate mainly
to husband-wife relationship. Allah gives it great importance. The supremacy of the husband in family affairs is, at
the same time, conceded. This is because he is charged 'to
support, feed and clothe' the wife and speak to her 'words
of kindness and justice' and 'treat her gently'. The wife on
her part has to appreciate that the husband is a 'degree
higher than' her because as Allah explains in the Quran he
has to spend a part of his wealth on her and take care of the
financial burden of their offsprings. She has to give to the
husband not only love and care but also obedience because
that alone can ensure harmony in the family which is essential to keep the institution of family in tact for on it rest the
pillars of civilization.

"Man is biologically so constituted that he is apt to go
astray; his sexual passion has, therefore, to be contained.
Hence the Quran permits him to marry more than one wife:

    'Marry women of your choice
    Two or three or four; (4:3)

"But the permission is conditional: everyone of the wives
has to be treated justly — not only materially but also in
love and all other respects. The Prophet showed, by his
example, how this could be done; I need not recount it here
but none of his wives had any complaint against his treatment. He divided his time and attention equally between
them; he showered his affection and care equally on them.
For ordinary mortals this may not be possible. Hence the

admonition:

> "But if ye fear that ye shall not
> Be able to deal justly (with them)
> Then only one". (4:3)

Here again the Quran is clear and logical:

> "You shall never be able to do justice among wives, no
> matter how desirous you may be." (4:3, 128).

This is more ah admonition to practice monogomy than polygamy.

"Divorce has, no doubt, been made easy by the Quran for the husband; but that is because in case the wife loses his affection and care, life with him would be unbearable; divorce in such circumstances would be preferable to continued harassment and ill-treatment. It may not be a happy solution; but what is the alternative? The Prophet said, 'Of all the permitted things, the one I detest the most is divorce'. The wife also has been given the right under certain circumstances to divorce the husband; as the Quran says:

> If a wife fears
> Cruelty or desertion
> On her husband's part,
> There is no blame on her
> If she arranges an amicable settlement;
> And such settlement is best;
> Even though men's souls are swayed by greed. (4:128)

"It is reported that a woman came to the Prophet and pleaded that there was no love between her and her husband; hence she might be granted divorce. The Prophet asked her whether she would return whatever he gave her as dower. 'More than that', the woman replied. The Prophet said, 'There is no need to give anything more' and granted her the divorce.

"Another point that has been urged before us is about inheritance. Why has the Quran decreed to the male, 'a portion equal to that of two females'? Does it not show gross inequality between the two sexes? No. It takes a practical view of the financial burden that a male bears, as against a female, in a family; the male maintains the family; the female is not so required. She can spend her legacy as she likes, even her husband has no control over it. Further, she gets dower and inherits both from her father's and her husband's side.

In all these matters to which the Quran refers, the predominant factor is the preservation of the family; it has hardly any relation to the outside world. The Quranic verses which make a reference to a woman's behaviour with persons outside the family orbit, are not more than two.

"The first one is about restrictions on appearance:

'And say to believing women
That they should lower
Their gaze and guard their modesty;
That they should not display their
Beauty and ornaments except
What (must ordinarily) appear thereof;
That they should draw their veils over
Their bosom and not display their beauty except...'
(24:31)

But this admonition is no different from that contained in the preceding verse, which is addressed to men:

'Say to the believing men
That they should lower
Their gaze and guard their modesty;
That will make for greater purity for them;
And God is well acquainted
With all that they do'.   (24:30)

The second Quranic verse refers to the movement of women outside their homes:

'O Prophet! Tell
Thy wives and daughters

And the believing women,
That they should cast
Their outer garments over
Their persons (when abroad)
That is most convenient.
That they should be known
(As such) and not be molested
And God is oft — Forgiving,
Most Merciful'. (33.59)

My reverend Imam Bukhari has recorded in his *Sahih* that
the Prophet had told women that 'Allah has permitted you
to go out of your houses for genuine need'. Moving around
aimlessly is not favoured as it would not be safe for them to
do so; but there is no restriction on going out to work.
During the time of the Prophet women went out to buy
provision, to get water, to tend and nurse the wounded,
and on Fridays and Id days even to pray in mosques alongside with men. It is also proper that a woman should have a
mehrum or a male relative or guard, while travelling abroad;
that is only for her protection.

"Then there is the Quranic verse about the evidence of a
woman being half that of a man:

'And get two witnesses
Out of your own men,
And if there are not two men,
Than a man and two women
Such as ye choose,
For witnesses,
So that if one of them errs,
The other can remind her'. (2.282)

But this is specifically in respect of a financial transaction,
in which, women, by nature, are not adept. Also as a
protection to them — one woman could help to refresh the
memory of the other so that they may not be accused of
perjury.

"As against these verses, in which woman is not equal to
man, there are innumerable verses,   in which the equality

of the sexes, has been proclaimed:

> 'Whosoever works righteously
> Man or woman, and has Faith,
> Verily, to him will We give
> A new Life, a life
> That is good and pure, and We
> Will bestow on such their reward
> According to the best
> Of their actions. (16:97)

"Again there is the verse:

> Women impure are for men impure
> And men impure are for women impure
> And women of purity
> Are for men of purity
> And men of purity
> Are for women of purity:
> These are not affected
> By what people say:
> For them there is forgiveness
> And a provision honourable. (24:26)

"The Prophet showed the highest consideration to women; he always acted in accordance with the teachings of Quran, which, in verse after verse, has emphasised the equality of man and woman:

> And among His Signs
> Is this, that He created
> For you mates from among
> Yourselves, that ye may
> Dwell in tranquility with them,
> And He has put Love
> And mercy between your (hearts):
> Verily in that are signs
> For those who reflect'. (30:21)

"The Quran also makes it clear that the reward for man and

woman from God for the good deeds done by them is the same:

> Surely for men who submit to God and women who submit to God;
> For believing men and believing women;
> For devout men and devout women;
> For truthful men and truthful women;
> For steadfast men and steadfast women;
> For humble men and humble women;
> For charitable men and charitable women;
> For men who fast and women who fast;
> For men who guard their honour and women who guard their honour;
> For men who remember God and women who remember God;
> For them both God has assured forgiveness and mighty reward". (33:35)

"Hence except in family affairs, there is no specific injunction in the Quran which can lead us to conclude that woman has to be subordinate to man; to her husband, yes, but not to others. In fact, morally, she stands many times superior to man. In my book: *Mukashafatul Qulub*, I have narrated two incidents which prove that woman is instinctively more pious than man; she is more protective of her honour and the integrity of her family than man. She does not succumb to temptation as easily as man does.

"Once a young man got attracted to a beautiful girl; he followed her everywhere. She happened to go on a journey in a caravan; the young man also managed to get on it. When the caravan halted at night in some forest, he secretly came to the girl and begged her to sleep with him. She told him to make sure first that everyone was asleep. He went around and came back, assuring her that all were fast asleep. 'Are you sure?' asked the girl. 'I am positive' he replied. 'What about God', she enquired. 'Is He also asleep? Will He not see and punish us?' The young man was taken aback; he had no reply. He quietly went away.

. There is yet another instance; it is of a married woman whose husband was unable to provide food for her children; she went to a merchant to get them foodgrains and provisions. The merchant demanded his price in flesh. The woman begged of him not to force her into sin but he would not agree. She returned empty handed; the children were unable to bear the pangs of hunger. The husband had no means to satisfy them; he, therefore, goaded his wife to go back to the merchant, who was pleased to see her return. As she was about to give in, the fear of God gripped her. She started shivering. He asked her what was wrong. She said: 'How will I be able to face my Creator?' The man was non-plussed. He told her, 'Even in such distress you do not forget God!' He felt so ashamed that he gave her the foodgrains and the provisions and vowed to lead a moral life thereafter.

"In both cases I ask: who exhibited a greater sense of morality, honour and piety? The man or the woman? True, sometimes under economic stress, she gives in; that is how she turns into a prostitute. But in most cases it is the man who leads the woman astray. Left to herself she is pure as gold. That is why the Prophet declared that Paradise lay at the feet of the mother. He gave a much higher position to her than to the father. Once a Companion asked the Prophet whom should he obey most? The Prophet replied: 'The mother'. 'And after her', he asked. The Prophet replied, 'The mother'. The Companion persisted again; he got the same reply. It was the fourth time, that the Prophet told him: 'Then the father'. This is recorded by Imam Bukhari in his *Sahih*.

Hence there are spheres where a woman can be regarded as equal, even superior to man; whether these include politics and public affairs, we shall decide after we have heard the arguments of both sides.

Imam Shafi'i: The relationship between a husband and a wife is most sacred; it has to be guided by principles which will ensure its stability. The Quranic admonitions have to be understood in this spirit; the husband has, necessarily, an upper hand. He is the provider of the wife and the children; he is in other ways also the superior of the two. Polygamy is the result of this superiority; so also the greater liberty for divorce that the husband enjoys over the wife. However, this does not mean that the husband can ill-treat the wife. On the contrary, the Prophet made it clear that "the best of my followers is he who is fairest in his treatment of his wife." In his farewell address on the occasion of his last pilgrimage, he declared:

> O my people: You have certain rights over your wives and so have your wives over you ... They are Allah's trust in your hands. So you must treat them with utmost kindness.

On one occasion, the Prophet was on a journey with a lot of men and women. The camel drivers speeded, fearing the Prophet might be late for his destination. He cautioned them not to go fast and mind the crystal. By crystal he meant women, who are naturally delicate. There are many other Hadith, which point to the protection that women enjoyed at his hands. He did not consider them inferior but took them to be fragile. He was always anxious to safeguard their interest. The Quran has admonished husbands that even if they disliked their wives, they should be indulgent towards them because 'You may dislike a thing, in which Allah placed abundant good.' The other verses which permit husbands to beat their wives have to be read in conjunction with the verse just quoted by me to get a clearer picture of woman's position in Islam.

Imam Muslim: Though in marriage, a man has a higher position than a woman, it has to be a relationship of mutual consent and respect. Aisha, the Prophet's youngest wife, has quoted him to the effect that when she asked him whether a young virgin girl, could be given in marriage by her guardian without her consent, the Prophet said, 'No, she must be consulted.' Aisha asked what would happen, if being shy, she were not to respond. In that case, the Prophet said, her silence might be construed as her consent. According to another Hadith, narrated by a Companion of the Prophet, Abu Huraira, an unmarried woman, even if she is a widow or divorcee, could not be married unless she was consulted and she had given her consent. Again, there is a Hadith, narrated by another Companion, Alqama, who reported: While I was walking with Abdullah at Mina, Uthman met him. He asked why had he not married. Abdullah sought the Prophet's advice, who told him he should marry provided he could support a wife; otherwise he should fast occasionally to control his sexual urge, so that he might not go astray.' The Prophet's warning was always to men; never to women, who are rarely unfaithful or immoral unless forced by circumstances, beyond their control.

The other Imams endorsed generally the views of their colleagues, who had already spoken; the President, Imam Ghazali then adjourned the proceedings and said that from the following day, the Council would hear the evidence and the arguments on the final question: whether a woman can be the head of an Islamic government or state or not?

SECTION
IV

Can a Woman
be a Ruler?

8

The Crucial Evidence

Sixth Day

The Imams, headed by Imam Ghazali,entered the hall, Rashid Rida announced their arrival, the whole gathering stood up. As soon as the President and the other venerable members of the Council took their seats, the proceedings began.

Imam Ghazali, looked at A. K. Brohi, the counsel for the petitioners, and asked whether he was ready.

Brohi: Yes, Your Honour! We are grateful to you and the members of the Council for the clear elucidation of the status of woman in Islam. It has not been the contention of the petitioners that woman is inferior to man and that is why she cannot be a ruler in an Islamic state; our case is that she is different from man. Both are complementary to each other. Woman is meant for the home and man for the world outside. The veil is the symbol of that division and not a sign of bondage. I shall now, with your permission, call Sayyid Sulaiman Nadvi, a most learned man, whose works on Islam numbering about a hundred have acquired scholastic eminence. He has been the founder of many research institutes in India and was specially invited to preside over the Convention of the Ulama, representing every school of theology; it was held in 1951, at Karachi to formulate the fundamental provisions of an Islamic constitution. Twenty-three leading Ulama headed by Nadvi appended their signatures to the document. One of the questions they discussed was whether a woman could be the head of an Islamic state. They decided unanimously that she could not be and that it would always have to be a male Muslim in whose piety, learning and soundness of judgement the people or their elected representatives had confidence. There were many other provisions on which they dilated and expressed their opinion; but here we are only concerned with the question of the sex of the Head of State. May I ask you, Nadvi Saheb, why did you debar a woman from being the Head of State?

Nadvi: That is our understanding of the Quran and the traditions of the Prophet.

Brohi: Will you kindly explain it to this august Council?

Nadvi: I cannot do better than quote the view of the Board of *Talimat-e-Islamia* when this issue was referred to it by a sub-committee on federal and provincial constitutions of the Constituent Assembly of Pakistan. May I read it?

Imam Ghazali: Please do.

Nadvi: Here is the full text of their views on this question: "The Board have been asked to furnish the reasons and authorities, from the Shariat point of view, whereupon they have based their recommendation that the Head of the State must be of male sex. The following two verses will suffice to enable one to understand the Quranic viewpoint in regard to men and women and the superiority of the one over the other notwithstanding their equality in certain respects:—

a) 'Men are in charge of women, because Allah hath made the one of them to excel the other. ' (4:34).
b) 'And they (women) have rights similar to those (of men) over them in kindness, and men are a degree above them. ' (2:228)

· "Evidently when it has not been allowed that women folk should lead, dominate and wield ultimate authority in the domestic affairs, how can it be considered permissible in respect of the much wider domain of state politics. To ignore the basic viewpoint and to make a woman the final authority and thereby reverse the relation between the superior and and the subordinate is tantamount to a flagrant contravention of the Quranic view. Furthermore, it is one of the duties and functions of the Head of an Islamic state to lead Juma (Friday) prayers and Id prayers which is impossible for a woman to perform. The question of this office being held by a woman is, therefore, ruled out.

'The provisions of the Quran in regard to the evidence of women furnishes a further proof of the superiority of men in such matters and this provides another reason as to why a woman cannot be entrusted with the office of the Head of State. According to a Quranic verse:

> 'And call to witness, from among your men, two witnesses. And if two men be not (at hand) then a man and two women' (2:282)

'According to two traditions of the Prophet, it is the most unfortunate day for a nation when the reins of authority go into the hands of a woman:

> a) 'A nation that appoints a woman as its ruler shall never prosper'. (Bukhari)
> b) 'When the best from amongst you are your rulers, the rich from amongst you are liberal and the affairs of your State are decided upon by consultation among yourselves, then the surface of the earth is better for you than its inside. And when the worst among you are your rulers, the rich among you are miserly and the affairs of your State are entrusted to women, then the inside of the earth is better for you than its surface'. (Tirmidhi)'

Imam Ghazali: In this long extract, has the Board put all the arguments against a woman being a ruler?

Nadvi: I would like to also request you to peruse pages 5 and 6 of the Board's report dated June 1, 1950, which may be of some use in this context; it has been clarified therein that such discriminatory provision in no way implies any sort of degradation of women-folk. As a matter of fact, according to Islam, it is quite inevitable for the progress and prosperity of mankind that men and women do perform their own respective functions as ordained by nature itself, according to their respective faculties and aptitudes.

Imam Ghazali: I don't think verse 34 in surah Nisa(6) is of a general nature; it refers more to treatment of a woman in bed and hence seems to pertain to a husband's attitude to his wife.

Nadvi: So the Council has held; but many of us feel that the two parts of the verse are severable.

Imam Ghazali: Likewise, verse 228 in surah *al-Baqara* refers to divorce and the consequence thereof.

Nadvi: That is so, but this particular sentence has a general import.

Brohi finished his examination-in-chief. Ameer Ali got up and requested the Council to permit his associate, Yahya Bakhtiar, the Attorney General of Pakistan, to cross-examine Nadvi as Bakhtiar was more familiar with the developments in Pakistan. Imam Ghazali nodded his approval.

Bakhtiar: Nadvi Saheb, from your published works, which are of such a monumental nature, I gather that you have a most liberal approach to most controversial issues; why are you so rigid when it comes to women?

Nadvi: It is not a question of being rigid, we had to arrive at a consensus and, therefore, some compromise was inevitable.

Bakhtiar: Do you mean to say that left to yourself, you would have agreed to allow a woman to be the head of a government? You have, if I remember correctly, written glowing accounts of the achievements of Muslim women in one of your books.

Nadvi: I am committed to the consensus, that is the Islamic way of resolving a dispute.

Bakhtiar: Are you aware that this view of the Board of Ulama was rejected by the sub-committee of the Constituent Assembly of Pakistan on the ground that the Quranic verses were not relevant to the particular issue and further that the two Hadith or traditions of the Prophet relied upon by it were rather weak?

Nadvi: Yes, I am aware.

Bakhtiar: Are you also aware that the sub-committee asked the Board to provide it with more cogent and relevant grounds for incorporating the provision that only a male Muslim could be the Head of an Islamic state? It specifically asked for clear authorities and not interpretative comments. To quote its words: "It was necessary to know whether it was one of the fundamental principles of Islam."

Nadvi: Yes.

Bakhtiar: And also that no such principles were forwarded by the Board to the sub-committee?

Nadvi: Soon thereafter, many unexpected and unfortunate developments took place in Pakistan and all such issues got buried in the debris of events.

Brohi then requested the Council to allow him to recall Maududi. Imam Ghazali consented.

Brohi: Why have you held that a woman cannot be a ruler in an Islamic state?

Maududi: Because I believe she is meant to look after her home. If she were to become a ruler, she would have no time for her children who need all her attention and care. That is why I am against any post of responsibility being given to a woman, whether it is presidentship, prime ministership, ministership, or even membership of parliament or any legislature or directorship of any establishment. I believe that in Islam there is a functional distribution of work between man and woman and in accordance with this distribution, politics and administration come within man's sphere of activities.

Bakhtiar cross examined Maududi.

Bakhtiar: Is it a fact that you had supported Fatima Jinnah, the sister of Quaid-i-Azam, against Ayub Khan in the election for the presidentship of Pakistan in 1962?

Maududi: Yes, but that was an exceptional case.

Bakhtiar: Who decided that it was so?

Maududi: I did; every man has to use his own judgement in order to take a decision for his actions.

Bakhtiar: And what were those exceptional circumstances?

Maududi: Ayub had assumed such dictatorial and oppressive powers that no one could have defeated him except Fatima Jinnah because of her mass popularity and the esteem in which she was held generally as the sister of the founder of Pakistan.

Bakhtiar: So it was expediency and not adherence to any rule of the Shariah that made you support Fatima Jinnah?

Maududi: That is not correct; the Quran even allows eating the prohibited meat like pork if necessity so demands.

Bakhtiar: The circumstances which brought Benazir to power were worse; Zia had corrupted the state; throttled democracy; manipulated judiciary; murdered his predecessor; sent thousands of innocent Muslims to jail; unleashed a reign of terror...

Zia-ul-Haq, who was sitting quietly in one corner, got up and as was his wont spoke in a controlled and humble manner. "That is not at all correct, my Imams. I am a God-fearing man. I am a practising Muslim. I did not kill Zulfiqar Ali Bhutto. I only carried out the judicial verdict of the Supreme Court. I did not behave like a dictator; I have always been a humble man and anyone who came in contact with me is well aware of that. I had never aspired to be the President. I believed that Pakistan was created to be a truly Islamic state...."

Quaid-i-Azam Jinnah (1876-1948) got up and said: "Yes, a truly Islamic state; but certainly not a theocratic state, My Lords, which is what Zia-ul-Haq turned it into..."

"Why do you address the members of this Council as My Lords?" thundered Ihteshamul Haq. "As Muslims we cannot address anyone so, however much we may respect him. Muslims recognise only one Lord, the Almighty."

"I am sorry," said Jinnah, a little shaken by the Maulana's rebuff. "Habits die hard. Practising at the bar in India for many years, I got used to addressing judges as 'My Lords'. It is just a manner of speaking, Sir."

Imam Ghazali called for order: "We seem to be digressing from the basic issue; we are concerned only with the adjudication on the point whether Benazir, as a woman, can continue as Prime Minister of Pakistan. We have not gathered here to pronounce our verdict on the rule of Ayub Khan or Zia-ul-Haq. So please address us only on the points at issue."

Brohi's last witness was S. Ameenul Hasan Rizvi, an Islamic scholar of repute. He has been editor of *Radiance*, a weekly journal of Jamaat-i-Islami of India. A lawyer by training, well versed in theology, Mr. Rizvi has the distinction of being a rational ideologue of the fundamentalist viewpoint.

Brohi: I gather from your writings that you are firmly of the view that a woman in Islam cannot be a ruler.

Rizvi: You are right! This issue cannot be looked into in isolation but in the context of the totality of Islam's approach to the functioning of Muslim women in our society. From the days of Prophet Muhammad to the present times there has been unanimity among Islamic scholars that the sphere of a Muslim woman's activity is her home.

Imam Ghazali: I do no think that is a correct assessment; there are differing viewpoints.

Rizvi: I am referring to the classical jurists and not the modern rootless cosmopolitans, who derive their inspiration from the Orientalists.

Bakhtiar got up on a point of order and pointed out that the witness was trying to reopen the general issue, which had already been settled by the Council.

Imam Ghazali upheld the objection and asked Rizvi to confine himself to the particular issue before the Council.

Rizvi: My Imams, I live in the same times as Benazir Bhutto. I have been a witness to her rise to power. I wish I had not lived to see it. Every day I read of her activities in the press and I feel ashamed. Islam does not expect its women to conduct themselves in this manner. The Quranic injunctions are clear; are they being observed by Benazir? The way she functions — and I suppose she has no choice — as the Prime Minister of Pakistan does not fit into the Islamic framework. She is constantly exposing herself to men through her regular presence in the National Assembly, answering questions and making speeches, presiding over cabinet meetings, holding conferences with officials, talking to the President, or to one or the other male minister or a male secretary to government in complete seclusion for confidential discussions, attending State banquets at home and abroad and proposing toasts to various male dignataries, mixing freely with them, exhibiting herself in public and at government functions, talking in absolute privacy, without any aids, to her male colleagues or subordinates at home and to male visiting foreign dignitaries both at home and abroad and also while on state visits to foreign countries. In short, every day she is more in the company of men and often in privacy or seclusion.

Imam Abu Hanifa: But if she covers herself properly and conducts herself with propriety, would you still consider it objectionable?

Rizvi: Yes my Imam, even then, I submit, it is a violation of Islamic rules and practices. There is no instance of our Prophet having allowed women to participate in politics or administration; allowing them to go out to mosques for prayers or to attend to the sick on the battlefields is different. The Hadith recorded by Imam Bukhari has to be understood in this context; it is a warning to the Muslims not to entrust the affairs of state to women because they would make a mess. The other Hadith by Imam Tirmidhi is much more explicit. I shall quote it in full:

"The Prophet is reported to have said that when your rulers are from the best among you, the well-to-do among you are charity-minded and your collective affairs are dealt with through mutual consultation, then the surface of the earth is better for you than its belly (meaning that life is worth living); but when your rulers are of evil nature, the well-off among you are miserly and your affairs are in the hands of women, the belly of the earth would be better for you than its surface.'

"There has also been a reference here to Bibi Aisha leading troops in the 'Battle of the Camel' but it should not be forgotten that she regretted her action later. This has been confirmed by no less a person than Hadarat Abdullah Ibn Abbas, acknowledged as one of the greatest Islamic jurists who lived through those times and had remained strictly neutral in the conflict. He had commented that it would have been more desirable for Bibi Aisha to have remained in her home than to have been on the camel's back."

Ameer Ali then cross-examined Rizvi: "You seem to be more dogmatic than even some of the classical jurists; if one were to follow your line of thinking there would be complete segregation between men and women. Is it practical or feasible in present times?"

Rizvi: My complaint is that the present times have degraded women and brought them to the nadir of moral degeneration and material corruption in the world. What we are witnessing is the flowering of the Kingdom of Satan. Ayatollah Khomeini was perfectly justified in describing both U.S.A. and U.S.S.R — the two super powers, controlling the world — as the Great Satans. What we have to strive for is the destruction of the rule of these Satans and to help usher in the Kingdom of God for which our Prophet worked and in which every true Muslim must believe.

Since Brohi had no more witnesses to examine, Bakhtiar called his first witness, Jamal-al-Din al-Afghani (1838-1897), the pioneer of Pan-Islamism in the nineteenth century. He advocated united action by the Muslims against the illegal and forcible occupation of their lands by the European powers. He has yielded considerable influence on young Muslims everywhere and at all times. Abduh was one of his distinguished pupils. Iqbal regarded him as the only modern intellectual who had deep insight into the maladies from which his co-religionists suffered and who had the learning and ability to reconstruct religious thought in Islam. He was also a great champion of women's emancipation.

Bakhtiar: Are you satisfied with the lot of Muslim women?

Afghani: Not at all. They are treated worse than chattels.

Bakhtiar: Are you in favour of their participating in public affairs?

Afghani: Absolutely. It is not Islam which debars them from such participation; but the Sassanid influence on Muslims which introduced the veil among women and kept them confined to their homes. Many of them in the past had actively taken part in the various battles that the Prophet fought in defence of his mission; some of them participated in the discussion of the *Shura* or the consultative council. Caliph Umar appointed a woman to one of the key posts in his administration, she was Shifa bint Abdullah who controlled the markets in Medina. The Prophet's youngest wife, Aisha was an active participant in major political developments. Muslim women in those days prayed in mosques along with men; they also accompanied their men for the Id prayers in congregations.

Bakhtiar: Was there no segregation of men and women?

Afghani: None at all. Every Muslim, whether male or female, was of course expected to behave decently. The Quranic injunction is clear on the point:

> ' O Prophet! Tell the believing men to restrain their eyes from looking at other women and guard their shameful parts; this is a pure way for them; surely, Allah knows what they do.'
> ' And O Prophet! Tell the believing women to restrain their eyes from looking at other men and guard their shameful parts. ' (24:30-31)

Further, men are strictly warned by the Quran:

> 'Those who desire to spread indecency and obscenity among the believers have a grievous torment in store for them, in this world and the hereafter '. (24:19)

Hence the Islamic approach is the same towards men and women. In fact men are told to be more careful in their public behaviour.

Bakhtiar: So you feel that the shutting of women from politics or affairs of state cannot be justified on the basis of Islamic tenets?

Afghani: I see no justification either in the Quran or the traditions of the Prophet and even in early Islam; this was a subsequent development under which the rulers who were all men kept women under subjugation. That is why Muslims have lagged behind in the race of civilization; and hence their progress continued to be thwarted. I am firmly of the opinion that it will be impossible for us to emerge from this humiliation and distress, from the depths of ignominy as long as women are deprived of their rights and not allowed to rise to their full stature and become equal partners with men in every activity, including politics and administration. I cannot express myself better than in the words of the great poet, Iqbal, who has attributed them so beautifully to me in his allegorical poem: *Javid Nama*:

Man alive in heart, do you know what thing life is?
One-seeing love that is contemplating duality:
man and woman are bound,one to the other,
they are the fashioners of the creatures of desire.
Woman is the guardian of the fire of life,
her nature is the tablet of life's mysteries;
she strikes our fire against her own soul
and it is her substance that makes of the dust a man.
In her heart lurk life's potentialities,
from her glow and flame,life derives stability;
she is a fire from which the sparks break forth,
body and soul, lacking her glow, cannot take shape.
What worth we possess derives from her values
for we are all images of her fashioning;
if God has bestowed on you a glance aflame
cleanse yourself, and behold her sanctity.

Bakhtiar concluded his examination-in-chief; Brohi then took over and cross-examined Afghani.

Brohi: You seem to have gone ahead of even the West in your demand for women's emancipation.

Afghani: Islam was always ahead of Christianity; it is the dye-in-the-wool theologians who have stultified its growth.

Brohi: But don't you see what emancipation has done to women?

Afghani: Why only women; why not look at what the West has done to men also. It is their hypocrisy which is the cause; they tend to talk of one thing and do another. In Islam there is no place for hypocrisy; what I ask for is equal opportunities for men and women. Once you concede these, Islam will keep them on the right path; it does not allow permissiveness among either men or women. And an awakened woman will be the best safeguard against a morally corrupt man.

Bakhtiar requested the Council to permit him to recall Allama Abdullah Yusuf Ali, the noted commentator of the Quran. On permission being granted, Yusuf Ali stepped into the witness box.

Bakhtiar: Your commentary on the Quran has been universally accepted in the Muslim world. May I ask you to refresh your memory and recapitulate the references in the Quran to Bilqis, the legendary Queen of Sheba.

Yusuf Ali: These references occur in *Surah Namal* (27) in verses 15-44.

Bakhtiar: Are they favourable to Bilqis, the Queen of Sheba?

Yusuf Ali: Yes, very favourable.

Bakhtiar: Can you tell us more about it?

Yusuf Ali: Saba was the name of the inhabitants of South Arabia. The capital city Ma'rib, was situated about 80 kilometers from the present Sanna, the capital of North Yemen. Saba were a flourishing people, adept in commerce; they reached the height of prosperity during the reign of a woman, named Bilqis, the legendary Queen of Sheba. During the same period (about 1100 to 800 B.C.) there ruled over the present Palestine, Jordan, the West Bank and part of Syria, Solomon who was mightier than any ruler of his times. He was a good and virtuous man who believed in one God and always followed the righteous path. He was, in fact, a prophet and the son of Prophet David. His army, according to the Quran, consisted of men, jinns and birds. One day he found one of his favourite birds, called Hoopie, missing; on enquiry Solomon was told that it had just returned, bringing information about another kingdom where people worshipped the sun but whose ruler was a noble lady, ever solicitous of the welfare of her subjects. She ruled by consulting her Council, consisting of the local leaders.

Bakhtiar: What happened next?

Yusuf Ali: Solomon wrote a letter to Bilqis, inviting her in the name of God, the Compassionate and the Merciful, to refrain from worshipping anyone else except God and choose the true path.

Bakhtiar: What was the Queen's response?

Yusuf Ali: She was rather puzzled; it was an unusual invitation. She consulted her Council; some of them suggested war but most of them wanted her to spurn the offer. However being sagacious and wise, she decided to send her envoy to Solomon, with an array of gifts, to mollify Solomon and earn his goodwill.

Bakhtiar: What was Solomon's reaction?

Yusuf Ali: When the envoy presented the gifts to Solomon, he angrily threw them away, saying he was not after wealth but was only interested in spreading the divine message of truth. The envoy conveyed Solomon's reaction to the Queen, who then decided to go personally to Soloman. He was happy to receive the Queen, and when she arrived in his palace, she was amazed to see her own throne installed there. At first she thought it was an imitation, but the moment she came close to it, she realised that it was her own throne. The miracle was due to God's grace, Solomon told Bilqis. Overwhelmed by the power of God, the Queen embraced the true faith.

Bakhtiar: What is the moral of this story?

Yusuf Ali: That a good and virtuous person, whether male or female, does not resist the divine call and surrenders himself or herself spontaneously to God and takes to the true path.

Bakhtiar: I am thankful to you.

Brohi then got up to cross-examine Yusuf Ali.

Brohi: What has this story to do with the question whether a woman can be a ruler or not?

Yusuf Ali: Had Bilqis not been a wise ruler, she would not have responded to Solomon's invitation to choose the true path and to discard the false one which she realised would have brought disaster to her people, sooner or later.

Brohi: Is this not your inference that she was a wise ruler?

Yusuf Ali: No. The following words of the Quran, throw ample light on her conduct as the ruler:

"The queen said, 'O chiefs, a very important letter has been cast before me. It is from Solomon, and it begins with the name of Allah, the Merciful, the Compassionate. It says, do not adopt a rebellious attitude against me and present yourselves as Muslims before me'."

Having read out the letter the queen said, 'O chiefs, counsel me in this matter; I do not take a decision in any matter without (consulting) you.' They replied, 'We are a powerful people, and good fighters. The decision, however, rests with you. You may yourself consider as to what command you should give.' The queen said, 'When the

kings enter a land, they ruin it and debase its honourable
people. I shall send to him gifts with my envoys and then
wait and see with what reply they return.

Ameer Ali then craved the Council's indulgence to call
Aminah al-Said who had been in the forefront in Egypt in
the movement for women's liberation. A prolific writer, she
had been editing *Hawwa*, a weekly magazine, devoted to
the uplift of Muslim women. She has authored many
books, championing the cause of women's rights. She was
actively connected with the press and travelled widely
throughout the world.

Ameer Ali: What kind of liberation of women are you
aiming at — western or Islamic?

Aminah: I don't follow this question; by liberation we
mean the same rights for men as for women. We are not
interested in semantics. In fact, I feel that while the woman
in the West was struggling to survive, her Muslim counter-
part, daughter of the empty sands and the primitive society, was enjoying life as a human being, exercising the same
rights as man. The Prophet lifted her from the slough of
degradation in which she lay and gave her a position of
respect and honour. However, with the decay that set in
during the subsequent periods, man regained his supremacy in Islamic society and the Muslims, who were the
innovators of women's rights, became the perpetrators of
the worst kind of inequalities against them, what with the
establishment of the *harem* and the resort to polygamy and
instant divorces. My complaint is that Muslims stopped at
the magnificent beginning that the Prophet made and did
not enhance the status of woman further in the spirit of the
teachings of the Prophet.

Ameer Ali: So we have remained at the stage where the
Prophet left us.

Aminah: No, as a matter of fact, we have gone back, in
many ways, to the dark ages before Islam. And the West
took up the cause of women's emancipation from the point
where our Prophet had left it. Muslims are the predeces-
sors; the westerners are the successors. They moved with
the times, but we stayed behind. The result is that Muslims
have lagged behind in the race of civilization while the

westerners are marching ahead.

Ameer Ali: How did this happen?

Aminah: Our society refused to move with the times, though the Quran enjoins upon us to do so. Not only that, our theologians made a virtue of old social beliefs and dogmas and resisted reforms on the basis that everything that they decreed had divine sanction. Unfortunately, hardly anyone protested against this obscurantism. Thus they were encouraged to take our women backward, little realising that such backwardness cast dark shadows across spiritual values. And what is the end result of it? The Muslim woman has lost all that she had gained. She has been reduced to the same degradation as when the Prophet had found her. Alas, his life's mission has been wasted.

Ameer Ali: Is there any improvement in their lot now?

Aminah: There has been some improvement as far as the upper class, and, to a small extent, the middle class women are concerned; they are better educated than before. They work in different sectors, they contribute to the economic well-being of their families, and thus they are able to prove that they can be a great asset to men; but the women in the rural areas who constitute almost 70 per cent of the female population are in a terrible state; they are illiterate, poor, miserable and completely at the mercy of men.

Ameer Ali: Is the western woman really happy?

Aminah: She is undoubtedly happier than the woman in any other part of the world. She has become more useful to society. Oh there are, I admit, many pitfalls but on the whole she is much better-off than before. And, this became possible because of the industrial revolution which gave opportunities for her economic betterment. Unfortunately, these changes came so fast that our men have not been able to adjust to them; that is why the resistance. In some Muslim countries laws were passed to conform to these changes in the status of women; but general acceptability is yet to come. The result is the conflict between the old traditional norms and the new revolutionary ideas.

Brohi queried Aminah on cross-examination.

Brohi: You have talked of conflict between the old and the new; but is not this conflict the same as between spiritualism and materialism, which can never be resolved?

Aminah: I don't think women's liberation is anti-spiritualism or pro-materialism. It is a struggle for the survival of her soul. Our theologians have always looked down upon women, they have condemned the demand for their rights as preposterous.

Brohi: And by your struggle for equal rights, will you achieve salvation?

Aminah: Salvation rests with God; but I have, no doubt, that we will get more and more rights as Muslim society changes from a backward, agricultural society to a progressive, industrial one, which will eventually change the old belief that women are the weaker sex; it will then be known that they have more to them than just being able to bear and raise children. Why, even animals do this fairly competently! Our fight, reverend Imams, is certainly not with the Quran but its faulty interpretations; it is not with the traditions of our Prophet, who was the greatest liberator of women, but with their distortions by the classical jurists, who were the henchmen of the male chauvinistic ruling cliques all though the ages.

Imam Ghazali went into consultation with his colleagues in the Council; he then told the counsels for Benazir, Ameer Ali and Yahya Bakhtiar, that the Council would like to re-examine Benazir. They would like to be satisfied about her ability and capacity to manage the affairs of an Islamic state. Apart from the main question whether a woman can be a ruler in an Islamic state which has been so violently contested, there were other aspects, which might have a bearing on the determination of this issue.

Imam Ghazali: Before we hold that a woman can be a ruler, we would like to be satisfied that Islam is safe in her hands.

"Why is this test necessary for a woman only? Has it ever been applied to a man, Your Honour?" enquired Ameer Ali.

"No. May be you are right; but a woman in this position seems to be an exception to the general rule," replied Imam Ghazali.

Brohi jumped from his seat: "I entirely agree my reverend Imams: we are firmly of the view that in view of her young age, inexperience, lack of a proper Islamic training, her general indifference to the tenets of Islam, her bias towards western ideas and her rather free and unrestrained style of living, Benazir is indeed most unsuitable for the leadership of the Government of Pakistan."

Ameer Ali: We are ready for the test, Your Honour, but Benazir may be allowed the fullest opportunity to present her case and to show by comparison what was done to Islam in Pakistan in the past and what she proposes to do in the future to advance its cause. A comparative analysis is vital for such a determination.

Imam Ghazali: Have you any objection to that, Brohi?

Brohi: As a matter of principle, no , but it will depend on how she conducts herself in the witness box.

Ameer Ali: What does my friend mean by that?

Brohi: Well, in case Benazir Bhutto makes unfounded allegations and casts aspersions on others, Your Honour, we cannot allow her to proceed unchallenged; we shall have to defend ourselves.

"We shall see how it goes", remarked Imam Ghazali, and adjourned the proceedings for the day.

9

Benazir's Deposition

Seventh Day

Yahya Bakhtiar requested Benazir Bhutto to step into the witness box. She complied.

Imam Ghazali: Do you think you will be able to advance the cause of Islam, if we hold that you can continue to be the Prime Minister of Pakistan?

Benazir: I will be able to do it far better, my reverend Imam, than my predecessor who, in the name of Islam, did incalculable harm to our great religion.

Brohi: I object, Your Honour! Let her talk of herself and leave Zia-ul-Haq alone.

Benazir: I wish I could. But he is the cause of my coming to power. Had it not been for his misdeeds, this whole matter of a woman becoming the Prime Minister in Pakistan would not have arisen. I never wanted to be one; I would have been quite content to work in the bureaucratic set-up or perhaps on some diplomatic assignment.

Imam Ghazali: Please proceed with your reply to our question and avoid any personal aspersions against any one.

Benazir: I am not casting any personal aspersion against Zia-ul-Haq Your Honour: I am talking of his policies and his style of functioning which alienated him from the people. His autocratic rule brought nothing but disgrace to Islam.

Brohi: I am afraid this is going too far; this is unbridled character assassination! I beg for the protection of the Council. Benazir Bhutto must be asked to state her viewpoint and not indulge in charges and accusations with which this Honourable Council is not concerned.

Imam Ghazali: He is right; we are sitting here not to judge Zia-ul-Haq or his rule; we are only concerned with

Benazir and her capacity as a woman to be a ruler.

Benazir: As you please, my Imam; but I hope you will permit me to tell you of the state of affairs that existed in Pakistan after eleven years of martial law. After all, unless you know what I have inherited, I will not be able to explain to you the task I am engaged in and what I propose to do in the future.

Imam Ghazali: You may proceed.

Benazir: When I took over the affairs of the state of Pakistan as Prime Minister, I found everything in doldrums; there was no democracy, no independent judiciary, no free press, not even an impartial civil service. The army and the police were exploited for perpetuating a system, which had brought nothing but harassment to innocent citizens and untold misery to the poor and the downtrodden.

Brohi: These are generalisations, almost like in a schoolgirl's essay.

Benazir: All right. Let me be specific and I hope, Your Honour, Mr. Brohi will restrain himself and not interrupt me.

Imam Ghazali: Please proceed.

Benazir: May I ask whether bribery, corruption and nepotism are not regarded as sins in Islam?

Imam Ghazali: Of course they are.

Benazir: Then let me tell you, Sir, that in Zia-ul-Haq's regime, with all the talk of Islamisation, these vices had become so rampant that when I took over the administration, I did not know where to begin in order to stem the rot. The promotions in the armed forces were done not on merit but through influence; I retired dozens of officers prematurely and appointed to those posts merited persons The policemen used all kinds of methods to get posted in places where they could make the maximum amount of money by corrupt practices. The Customs — this being one of the most lucrative sectors — attracted the brightest young people to it because the pay-offs were the highest. A new class of entrepreneurs was smuggling everything into the country, from air conditioners, video equipment, refrigerators and television sets to the most ordinary every day requisites. They paid their way through Customs and then sold the items on the black market. Our State Bank has, after investigation, reported that nearly one-sixth of Pakistan's economy was controlled by black marketeers who paid no taxes.

The Afghan war corrupted our economy further. Arms meant for the *mujahideen* were smuggled out of Pakistan and sold in the black market; they were even sold inside Pakistan to anti-social elements, with the result that people were frightened to travel on the road after dark as bandits armed with automatic weapons looted them. There was no law and order; landowners and industrialists maintained private armies to protect their estates. The worst was the drug traffic; it had grown to such dimensions that Pakistan, the premier Islamic state had become the major supplier of heroin to the rest of the world. Inside Pakistan, more than a million young Muslims became addicted to it. You have just to look at the huge, ostentatious, garish mansions in Lahore, Karachi and in tribal territories to realise how their owners have shamelessly ruined the economy and the youth to enrich themselves. This was the effect of the so called "Islamisation" of Pakistan which gave these people the cover to hide their misdeeds and terrorise the people. Most of the religious leaders — the mullahs — were hired by them; they became their swords, but proclaimed themselves as the 'swords of Islam'. These are the hard facts, which no one can deny.

Brohi: But what had Islamisation to do with this; did any Islamic law give them the liberty or licence to indulge in such crimes?

Benazir: Under the cover of "Islamisation", these crimes were committed and none dared to touch the culprits because the elite, mind you, consisting of men, controlled the administration. Every measure, whether the Hudud Ordinances or the evidence law or the zakat rules, or the administrative directives; each of these measures was misused to perpetuate an unjust system.

Brohi: If she regards these measures as unjust Your Honour, then is she not challenging the Shariah itself?

Benazir: Shariah is pure as gold; it is the adulteration of it which has done the harm. I shall give, my Honourable Imams, a few examples to bring my point home. To implement the Hudud Ordinances, Shariah courts, consisting of dubious judges, were established. They dealt with such crimes as theft, adultery, rape, etc. One of the cases, which came before a Shariah court was that of Bibi, a blind servant girl, who gave birth to a child after she was raped by her employer and his son. They were charged with the offence; but she could not produce four eye-witnesses. The two men, therefore, went free while the blind girl was convicted of adultery and sentenced to public lashing and three years of imprisonment. There was an international outcry and the girl had to be freed. Is this Islamic justice?

There was the case of a twenty-four-year old Roshan Jan, who moved a Shariah court for divorce, alleging physical torture by the husband. She then left her home (as required by the ordinance) and moved into a neighbour's house. Her husband lodged a complaint with the police, accusing her of committing adultery with the neighbour, who was a married man. On the basis of this complaint, Roshan Jan was arrested. I don't know what happened to her; but this is not a solitary instance. The *Muslim* of Islamabad had reported that there were dozens of Muslim women kept in jail without trial and men were sexually abusing them.

I ask, my reverend Imams, what kind of Islamic justice is this? Is that the reason why men want women to be veiled and kept away from politics and administration? I can quote several such instances of how innocent women were harassed, persecuted and jailed in the name of Islam by the men who governed them.

Imam Ghazali: What do you intend doing as Prime Minister? Will you debar all men from administration?

Benazir: Not at all, my Honourable Sir; as a woman my sense of justice is far stronger than that of a man in my position. God has given us, as you yourself have pointed out, a much stronger sense of morality. I will try and present Islam in its proper perspective. Islam is, as one of its bitterest critics H. G. Wells has said, 'the broadest, freshest and cleanest political idea that had yet come into actual activity in the world and it offered better terms than any other to the masses of mankind.' The whole process of the so-called 'Islamisation' in Pakistan was misconceived. It was made most oppressive.

Brohi: If the system was really so oppressive, how is it that despite the opinion of so many Ulama, that a woman should not participate in politics, you were allowed to contest the elections and were even appointed Prime Minister?

Benazir: I will answer your question. It was soon after my return to Pakistan, that a new ordinance was promulgated, I think in June 1988 — under which any law — even a constitutional provision — could be set aside by a Shariah court. The timing was significant. The press throughout the world had speculated that it was a device to disqualify me as a woman to stand for the election. However, public opinion in the country was so overwhelmingly in my favour that the whole plan misfired. Then another plan was devised; the dates of the elections were so fixed as to prevent me from participating in them. I was going to have a baby. The period of my pregnancy was calculated by the Government and then the election dates were announced so as to coincide with the time of my delivery. However, Allah willed otherwise, and so the dates, though inconvenient, did not prevent my active participation in the campaign. Men are supposed to be the helpmates and protectors of women; but in my case they used every device to obstruct and damage me.

Brohi: Would you say this of your husband as well? Is that the reason why even after marriage, you continue to be called Benazir Bhutto and not Benazir Zardari. Zardari, my Imams, is the surname of Benazir's husband.

Benazir: Mr. Brohi has mocked at my western style of living; but how little does he know of the Islamic way. Let me remind him that it is in the West that the woman after marriage changes her name and takes the surname of her husband. In Islam the wife retains her maiden name. That is one more proof of equality between man and woman in Islam.

Brohi: Don't you think you are neglecting your child, your husband and your home, which should be your prime concern instead of pursuing this lust for power?

Benazir: Mr. Brohi will not succeed in provoking me. My reverend Imams, I can tell you I have no lust for power. When I returned home after studying at Harvard and Oxford, I looked forward to a happy, comfortable stay with my parents and my brothers and sister. But within weeks of my return, Zia staged the coup and arrested my father, the first popularly elected leader of the country. Zia was afraid of my father's hold and the popularity of his Pakistan People's Party. So he decided not to allow a single Bhutto to rest in peace. From the moment of my father's arrest until the time of his judicial murder and even thereafter, it was a long saga of torture for me, my mother, my brothers and sister. He jailed me under obnoxious conditions; he put me and my mother in solitary confinement for long years; he heaped every kind of insult and injury on us; finally he exiled me for over two years. And all along, in order to stay in power, he had let loose a reign of terror in the country.

All this made the people of Pakistan turn to me for succour. They looked to me for leadership to bring an end to the authoritarian rule. The more Zia persecuted me, the more ardent was the peoples' support for me. When I returned to Pakistan after two years of exile in April 1986, more than a million of my countrymen came out to greet me, asking me to take on the dictator. What should I have done in the circumstances, my Imams? Should I have turned my back on them? Should I have let them down? Would that have been an Islamic act?

Earlier, when my father was languishing in prison while the regime was trumping up charges against him in order to send him to the gallows, should I have merely sat back with folded hands? Would I have been a good Muslim then? No Your Hónour, I was just left with no choice; I had to fight for justice for my father and I had to take up the cudgels on behalf of the people and fight the Zia regime. And I did just that.

Brohi: Why did you marry then? You cannot have it both ways.

Benazir: When I was a student at Harvard and Oxford I often wondered why a woman needed a husband. She was capable of earning herself, I thought, and doing a job as good as a man. But I must confess that I was wrong. I now realise that a good marriage is a tremendous source of strength to a woman. The greater the burden she carries the more she needs an understanding companion. My husband, though I don't see him as often as I would like to, gives me a great deal of strength — the very fact that he is there by my side is emotionally very important to me. A woman needs such support much more when she faces the outside world than when she is just confined to the four walls of her home. The world is changing fast, my Imams; women cannot remain in isolation anymore. And why should they? Are men leading the same kind of life as their ancestors did? Are our mullahs functioning as the Companions of the Prophet did in seventh century Arabia? Is Mr. Brohi dressing, eating, socialising in the same way as his forebears did. He and his friends enjoy the modern lifestyle of the West but they resent if for their sisters. Why? Should women also not benefit from the advances that science has made? Our beloved Prophet brought about the greatest change in human history. He uplifted women — and gave them more than they could have ever dreamt of. I am no feminist, my Imams, but I believe that in man-woman relationship, we must try and strike the right balance so that both may be happy. As man progresses, so should woman. That is the need of the hour.

Brohi: The right balance is that your husband should be the Prime Minister and you should look after him and take care of your child at home.

Benazir: There he goes again, my Imams; as the Quran has said how can the seeing and the blind be the same.

"The central point of Islamic teaching Benazir has missed," interjected Sayyid Qutb, (1906-1966) the ideologue of Muslim Brotherhood, whom Nasser had hanged because of his involvement in an attempt to murder the then Egyptian President, "and that is whether she should devote her time as a mother to look after her son or spend it in ruling a country. Is the child of no importance?"

"He is most important to me; but my mother and husband look after him, when I am not with him," answered

Benazir.

"No one can replace a mother; her place is unique" asserted Sayyid Qutb. "No father, no grandmother, no nurse, no servant."

"Does that mean that all that a woman should do is to procreate and spend her life taking care of the children?" asked Ibn Rushd (1126 – 1198), one of the greatest Muslim philosophers who brought enlightenment to Europe, when it was groaning in the dark. His contributions were so varied that they extended from religion to medicine. Ibn Rushd continued, "a woman is, therefore, placed at the service of her husband and relegated to the position of procreation, rearing and breast feeding. But this makes her useless... more than half the Muslim population just becomes a burden on men, adding to poverty and retarding progress."

Imam Ghazali admired Ibn Rushd for his erudition; but he felt his remark was more a Greek thought than an Islamic belief.

Abdullah al Badawi (1801 – 1873), who is regarded by the Muslims as the best commentator of the Quran, got up and requested to be heard.

"Most certainly," said Imam Shafi'i.

Badawi said: "My reading of the Quran is clear; Allah has preferred man over woman in the matter of mental ability and good counsel and in his capacity to perform duties and for carrying out the divine commands. Hence, to man has been confined prophecy, religious leadership, sainthood, pilgrim rites, the giving of evidence in the courts, the obligations of *jehad*, participation in congregation prayers. Also, the privilege of electing chiefs...."

"Does it mean that women should not participate in the election of a chief?" Imam Muslim asked.

"That is my understanding," replied Badawi.

"I am of the same view," said Maududi.

"But Maududi's own disciples have given up this stand in Pakistan," pointed out Bakhtiar. "They not only put up women for elections but several of them have become legislators. If a woman can become a legislator, Sir, why can she not become the leader of the legislators?" Maududi had no answer.

Ibn Taiymiyya, a disciple of Imam Hanbal and a highly respected *Mujaddid* or reformer, wanted to draw the attention of Imam Ghazali to the latter's work: *Nasihatul Muluk* (Counsel to Rulers), in which the distinguished Imam had listed 18 points against women, which showed that she was incapable of being a ruler.

Imam Ghazali corrected Ibn Taiymiyya, "These were the common perceptions, which I had listed; however the world has much changed since then."

Abu Muhammad Abdal Malik Ibn Khaldun, (1332 – 1406), one of the greatest historians, who is known in Muslim annals as the "Father of Historiography" got up to say something.

Imam Ghazali looked at him respectfully.

Ibn Khaldun asked if he could say something.

Imam Malik: We will be happy to hear you.

Ibn Khaldun: I just want to emphasise that the world never remains static; our Prophet was the greatest mover and shaker of the world. He changed it beyond recognition. Islam encourages both multiplicity and change; so does history. The Quran warns us: "God never changes the condition of a people unless they change it themselves." Ours is a brotherhood which does not believe in any form of inequality — tribal, racial or sexual.

In fact Islam came to level up things. The question, whether a woman can be a ruler or not — hardly arose in the past and hence it may not be proper to go back to the past to find the solution. The Council must decide on the basis of the changed situation and what is the best now in the larger interest of our body politic. My humble plea is: please do not resist change.

"Ibn Khaldun, my most venerable Imams, is right. It is high time we do so," thundered Muhammad Ibn Tumart (1077-1130), a religious teacher, who had assumed the title of al-Mahadi and established the theocratic kingdom of Muwahhidin in Arab Spain in the thirteenth century. He explained, "Even in my times I wrote a poem in which I said:
'There is the woman
My mother, sister, daughter

She stirs in me the most sacred emotions
How can the holy book regard her unworthy
This most noble, beautiful creature
Surely the learned have erred
To read this in the Quran'.

"I am aware of your contribution, Ibn Tumart. Your poem has stirred many", commented Imam Ghazali.

"I hope the Council will help us change our perception about women," remarked Ibn Khaldun.

"For better or for worse?", asked Maududi.

"Allah knows best," said Imam Ghazali and on that solemn note closed the proceedings and announced that they would assemble the next day to hear the arguments from both the sides.

10

Arguments and Counter-Arguments

Eighth Day

The Council assembled, as usual, at the appointed hour to hear the arguments. The President asked Brohi to proceed:

Brohi: The evidence from both sides, on the issue before the Council has been concluded. This, as my venerable Imams are well aware, is the issue of issues. The other two matters on which we debated earlier and on which you have adjudicated, were not, as such, the subject of this petition. The petitioners approached this honourable Council for a clear decision on whether a woman can be a ruler in Islam. I may, therefore, be permitted, on the basis of the evidence produced here, to put forth my arguments in support of the plea of the petitioner.

Imam Ghazali: There should be no objection to this; what have you to say, Bakhtiar?

Bakhtiar: I have no objection provided I am shown the same consideration by my learned friend to present my side of the case.

Imam Ghazali: Fair enough. Please go ahead, Brohi.

Brohi: May it please your venerable Imams. For a week we have heard distinguished persons, whose contributions to Islamic learning and theology have been outstanding, express their views on the status of woman in Islam. These eminent men have lived at different times and in different periods; they have dealt with varied situations; they were confronted with numerous problems; they have done monumental work in their times and have made significant contribution to our society. They command our respect even today. Their understanding of the Quran and the traditions of the Prophet has been deep; their interpretations, commendable; their views have been of great value to us.

I hope my learned friend will not contradict me when I state that most of them were firmly of the opinion that Islam accords the same respect to woman as man. The difference arises in our understanding of their respective functions. We, on this side, believe that man by nature is superior to woman; but this superiority is not of a master and a slave. It is a superiority where the man is responsible for the woman – for her welfare and for protecting her from the outside world; while woman acts as his companion and help-mate. Life will be incomplete without their mutual cooperation. I concede that except in family matters, there is no specific injunction in the Quran, which declares man being superior to woman, but the general tenor of its teachings leans in favour of man.

Bakhtiar   rose on a point of order and asked whether Brohi was not trying to reopen the issues already settled by the honourable Council.

Brohi: Not at all, what I am trying to press before this venerable Council is the fact that due to the biological and emotional differences that exist between a man and a woman, a woman is not suited to discharge the onerous responsibilities of governance; it requires a different kind of skill and stamina which she lacks. Politics is an extremely tricky business and man alone can handle it.

Bakhtiar: Do you want to suggest that governance or politics is a dirty business?

Brohi: No, but it needs a cool and dispassionate approach rather than an emotional one, and there can be no dispute that a woman tends to be highly emotional. The more serious a crisis, the more she is likely to lose her nerves. That is why, I submit, she stands disqualified for the business of governance. There is yet another point which needs to be considered. A ruler has to be level-headed and balanced at all times; his judgement should not be conditioned by the physical or emotional problems that he or she may be facing.at a given time. Now in the case of a woman, she has to go through, for instance, menstruation every month. The Quran has characterised it as a sort of sickness (2:222). This is accepted by modern science. Margaret Mead, the celebrated author of *Male and Female*, has pointed out that while a woman's work is keyed up to the cycle of menstruation and pregnancy, that of a man could be depended upon in any emergency, since men are subject to no such periodic rise and fall in capacity as women are. Menstruation, in particular, affects a woman greatly; for instance according to a well-known psychologist, a woman, while menstruating, drives a car slowly, becomes confused at crossings; she types hesitantly, striking sometimes the wrong keys. As an actress she acts indifferently, becoming temperamental; as a doctor she becomes less sure of her diagnosis. Havelock Ellis, the famous sexologist, has remarked that a woman, during menstruation, is more impressionable, suggestive and has less control over her system. Many women suffer from fits of ill temper or depression; they become impulsive, with the result that their judgement is marred.

Ameer Ali: I see, so menstruation disqualifies a woman does it? That is to say that a confused or even an unstable man can make a good ruler but not a menstruating woman?

Brohi: I hope my learned friend will stop interrupting me. He will have his say later. What I was trying to put forth was that the effect of menstruation is only one part of my argument; there are other aspects which are equally relevant. Take, for instance, motherhood which is basic to the functioning of a woman and in a way it encompasses her whole being. That is why our Prophet has said that Paradise lies at the feet of a mother. There has been a move, in certain quarters, to free women from child bearing, but has it ever succeeded? No. It never will. No woman feels fulfilled unless she becomes a mother; as a European scholar, Van de Velde has said, 'To be a woman means to have the desire to become a mother, both physically and mentally.' He admits that there are some modern women, who are averse to motherhood, but characterises this attitude on their part as a mere pose . He explains, 'The maternal instinct exists in spite of this. Wherever it is repressed because of some fashionable fad or because of decadence or love of pleasure, it will also be seen that such repression has its consequences sooner or later. A more than temporary repression of the mother instinct is, practically speaking, impossible' .

Bakhtiar (interrupting): If a man can be a father as well as a politician, why can't a woman be a mother as well as a politician?

Brohi: There is a vast difference between the responsibilities of a father and a mother; the mother fulfils every need of a child. That apart, take pregnancy; for nine months, the woman goes through physical and mental changes, which affect her entire outlook? She does not, cannot, remain the same person; her mind gets totally and quite naturally preoccupied. Is it possible for her then, during that period, to tackle the day to day problems of administration, which require one's complete attention and tremendous presence of mind? Will she be in a position then to face and resolve the national and international crises which a country may be confronted with?

After the birth of the child, comes the period of child rearing; Benazir has said that her baby is being looked after by a nurse. Is that a natural, proper or healthy solution? Havelock Ellis writes in his book, *On Life and Sex:* 'The idea has been put forward (first of all by Plato in the famous fifth book of his *Republic*) that the infant should be removed from its natural parents and placed in the hands of nurses skilfully trained in all the science and art of modern hygiene in general, and puericulture, in particular. Certainly it is possible to find innumerable parents who are completely and lamentably ignorant of this science and this art. This may be specially so in those lands of communistic tendency, like Soviet Russia, where the Platonic ideal is most commended. But to be content to leave the mothers in ignorance and to train up in the knowledge of the duties of maternity, a body of women who are not intended to be mothers, except for other women's children, seems a perverted attempt to escape the difficulty. It is not calculated to benefit, and still less to render happy, the real mothers, the artificial mothers or the children. '

Sigmund Freud, the father of modern psychology, describes the relative position of a man and a woman in no ambiguous terms. He writes: 'Women represent the interests of the family and the sexual life; the work of civilization has become more and more men's business; it confronts them with ever harder tasks, compels them to sublimations of instinct which women are not easily able to achieve. Since man has not an unlimited amount of mental energy at his disposal, he must accomplish his tasks by distributing his libido to the best advantage. What he employs for cultural purposes he withdraws to a great extent from women and his sexual life; his constant association with men and his dependence on his relations with them even estrange him from his duties as husband and father. Woman finds herself thus forced into the background by the claims of culture and she adopts an inimical attitude towards it.'

Then there is the menopause in a woman's life, between the age of 45 to 55, when certain biological changes take place in a woman. Her ovaries cease to function, which causes reactions in other ductless glands. Tissues loosen and ligaments increase, with the result that there is local atrophy of generative organs and endocrine imbalance, which in turn, results in certain mental and emotional disturbances in a woman. Her blood pressure rises, which also disturbs her normal functioning. During this period, it is difficult for a woman to tackle sensitive political problems or take major governmental decisions which may affect the lives of millions of people. Hence the risk involved is too great; affairs of state cannot be left to the vagaries of a woman who has to inevitably undergo such biological, emotional and mental stresses and strains.

Islam divides the sphere of activities between a man and a woman, and emphasises the difference, as reflected in our laws of marriage, divorce, inheritance and even evidence If women are given less than men in all these matters it is because of natural factors, and it is these natural factors, which I submit, disqualify a woman from being entrusted with the onerous responsibilities of governance. To rule a country needs enormous physical and mental stamina; a woman must not venture into it because nature has not endowed her with the attributes necessary for such a role.

Bakhtiar: If that were so the Quran would have specifically laid down the restrictions.

Brohi: There was no need for it. Man and woman are so constituted by nature that the restrictions are inherent in them; it has also been scientifically confirmed. The eminent American scientist, Prof. Howard, has proved that men are more objective, and women more subjective; that women are liable to fatigue more readily than men because of less haemoglobin in their blood. Not being physically as strong as men, they tend to be highly strung and succumb easily to nervous strain. All these tendencies disqualify a woman from being a ruler. She should not, therefore, be encouraged to compete with men in politics, which demands qualities entirely to the contrary of what she possesses. The famous poet, Rabindranath Tagore, has observed 'If a woman's nature were really the same as that of a man, it would be a superfluity, a mere tautology... If women acquire the view that sex difference is only physical and that mentally and spiritually they are of the same nature as men, and if they act on this assumption (thus giving life a one-sided masculine form) then our civilization would sink into utter confusion and chaos'. Similarly, Prof. Arnold Toynbee, the renowned historian, whose eleven-volume *Study of History* has become a classic, has opined, 'In history, the ages of disintegration were usually the ages when women had left the home'.

As you are aware, our Prophet according to one tradition is reported to have said that a woman's rule will bring no prosperity to the people and according to another tradition that under it death is preferable to life for the faithful. These are harsh words, indeed, but the truth needs to be faced. A woman is a blessing at home; she is likely to be a curse outside, and even worse if she takes to politics and the business of governance. Therefore my Imams, it would neither be in her interest nor in that of the people at large that she be allowed to rule.

My learned friend has waxed eloquent about the blessings of westernisation and spoke in glowing terms of women's awakening. I quote here from the latest interview that the Russian novelist, Solzhenitsyn, winner of Nobel Prize, has given to the American magazine *Time*, which is most revealing:

'There is technical progress, but this is not the same thing as the progress of humanity as such. In every civilization this process is very complex. In western civilizations-which used to be called western-Christian but now might better be called western-Pagan — along with the development of intellectual life and science, there has been a loss of the serious moral basis of society. During these 300 years of western civilization, there has been a sweeping away of duties and an expansion of rights. But we have two lungs. You can't breathe with just one lung and not with the other. We must avail ourselves of rights and duties in equal measure. And if this is not established by the law, if the law does not oblige us to do that, then we have to control ourselves. When western society was established, it was based on the idea that each individual limited his own behaviour. Everyone understood what he could do and what he could not do. The law itself did not restrain people. Since then, the only thing we have been developing is rights, rights, rights, at the expense of duty.'

I have done, my venerable Imams. I thank you for your indulgence and pray to Allah that He may show us the right path.

Ameer Ali rose slowly, turned towards the august Council and began his address.

Ameer Ali: My revered Imams. Both Brohi and I agree that Islam accords the highest respect to a woman; you have adjudicated that except in family matters, they are equal. Now Brohi has resorted to another ingenious device; he has made out a case that governance is beyond her capacity due to physical, mental and emotional factors. He has quoted several modern authorities in support of his contention and relied on a tradition of the Prophet that a country could not prosper under the rule of a woman. I shall deal first with the modern aspect of his argument. He has disqualified woman from being ruler due to certain biological factors, such as menstruation, pregnancy, menopause, or even motherhood. Now it is nobody's case that

God cast woman in the same mould as man. They are ofcourse different; as are all other species, animate or inanimate. It is their very physical juxtaposition which results in creation.

Does that mean that one is superior to the other? And how do physical features affect the mental calibre of a human being? My learned friend has advanced no authority, ancient, medieval or modern, to show that a woman is intellectually inferior to man. Women have not produced as many outstanding intellectuals as men because they have been deprived of the opportunities for thousands of years.

As for their so-called physical disabilities, may I know whether men are the embodiment of perfect health all the time? Are they also not subject to physical and emotional stress? And whoever described them as cool and calm? In fact they are more easy to lose their cool, more arrogant, self-righteous and ruthless than women. Besides, men are not as intense or dedicated to the task they take on as women are; they tend to be less resolute, less single-minded in their commitment to a job and perhaps even less capable of sustained hard work. You will therefore see women far ahead of men in the academic records of schools and universities. Are all these not *natural* disabilities that men are afflicted with? Do these traits not become natural handicaps which would incapacitate a ruler from functioning ideally?

As against the many European authorities quoted by Brohi, I would like to refer to John Stuart Mill's essay on *The Subjection of Women*. It is a penetrating analysis of woman's psychological make-up; it is written in his characteristic style; logical, clear-cut and factual; he points out that 'the principle which regulates the existing social relations between the two sexes — the legal subordination of one sex to the other — is wrong in itself, and one of the chief hindrances to human improvement; and that it ought to be replaced by a principle of perfect equality, admitting no power or privilege on the one side, nor disability on the other'.

Brohi: Mill is out of date, I have quoted the latest authorities.

Ameer Ali: If Mill is out of date, then what about Havelock Ellis, whom my learned friend has quoted? Is he not out of date? All right, then let me refer to two outstanding present-day authorities: one, the erudite author of the controversial book: *The Female Eunuch*, Germaine Greer; she marshals facts and figures with vigour and incisiveness and asserts that woman is no longer prepared to accept a cramped and stereotyped role in a masculine world. And the other is Allan Bloom, whose book, *The Closing of the American Mind* has been hailed as a masterpiece. He writes: 'And here is where the whole business turns nasty. The souls of men — their ambitious, warlike, protective character must be dismantled in order to liberate woman from their domination '. Without this dismantling, there is no hope for our women; too long have we relied on men to liberate women. None of our rulers have shown the vision or foresight of our Prophet; on the contrary they have under alien cultural influences in the past — whether Byzantine or Persian — chained our women; most of the Hadith attributed to our Prophet, were concocted in order to keep our women under subjugation.

Brohi: Where is the question of subjugation; we also subscribe to their freedom. It is only a difference in approach.

Ameer Ali: I do not want to cross swords with my friend Brohi again and again but what he is offering is lip sympathy; the reality is different.

My friend has waxed eloquent on the physical frailty and the emotional imbalance of a woman and tried to show how unsuitable she is to head a government. He has talked of menstruation and menopause and even pregnancy and motherhood as if these were illnesses that lead to instability. Besides, for a moment I thought I was appearing not before a judicial council but a medical tribunal. He has quoted several authorities in support of his contention. Most of what he said has been disproved. He seems to be out of touch with the latest medical research conducted by Masters and Johnson and others. Suffice it to say that woman is now held to be as fit for any work as man and thus should be treated on equal terms.

Brohi: I have shown to you, with the help of authoritative works, how the kind of equality that my friend is advocating is not feasible. There are natural impediments to it.

Ameer Ali: Science has so progressed that these so-called natural impediments are no longer valid; new devices of contraception which could help in better planning of families, better facilities for health and child care and treatment against depressive effects, if at all there are any, of menstruation or menopause are now available.

Experimental studies have established that masculinity and feminity are not mutually exclusive alternatives but a combination of traits, unevenly distributed among individuals of either sex. Hence any generalisation is baseless. As *Encyclopaedia Britannica* points out, 'Physically as well as psychologically, each person is a unique balance of characteristics that, if one so wishes, may be placed on a continuum, extending from maleness at one end to femaleness at the other, with a wide area of overlap at the centre...' The differences in traits and aptitudes between sexes have been highly exaggerated; it has happened because on a comparison it has been seen that men are more adept in certain arts and women, in certain others. This has led to the acceptance of certain criteria distinguishing the members of one sex from the other. These criteria are no longer valid.

Recent investigations have shown that masculinity and feminity are matters of degree rather than contrasting concepts at opposite poles, as they used to be thought of in the past'. Biologists and genetists are coming to the conclusion that most of the ingredients are common between men and women, albeit in different proportions. The *Encyclopaedia Britannica* observes that 'no statement can with any certainty be made about the origins of feminine or masculine personality traits beyond saying that psychosexual orientation appears to be the outcome of complex interactions among genetic, hormonal, and environmental factors whose relative importance in the whole process of character formation is impossible to ascertain; There is now universal acceptance of this view by biologically oriented scholars no less than by psychologists and sociologists.

That apart, may I ask, my Imams, whether they would

agree with Brohi that man is such an embodiment of virtues that the affairs of state are invariably safe in his hands? What does the history of the world show? That several male rulers have been ruthless, tyrannical, inhuman and mentally unsound! That Chenghiz Khan and Tamerlane were the worst scourges on the earth; that the atrocities committed by Hitler, Mussolini and Stalin in recent times are the blackest spots on our civilization. Their cruelties resulted in the massacre of millions of people under their rule. No woman ruler ever behaved in the brutal manner in which they did; no woman ruler could. She has, after all, a mother's heart; as she feels for her children, so she does for her subjects. As compared to the faults of the female rulers, those of male rulers are much worse. In our times there have been only four woman Prime Ministers — Golda Meir of Israel, Indira Gandhi of India, Bandernaike of Sri Lanka and Margaret Thatcher of Britain; none of them had been ruthless though some may have been autocratic in their style of functioning.

Take a look at the World of Islam. What did the male rulers do? Most of them brought nothing but disgrace to Islam. They abandoned the republican form of government, as visualised by the Prophet and instead introduced despotic and nepotistic systems. My Imams, if men have caused repression of the faithful and the suppression of the human race then is it not better that women, with their compassion and broad humanism, are, for a change, allowed to take over the reins in their hands?

Let us now, Your Honour, turn to the position of women in the Muslim world. The Quran makes it obligatory on them to learn, but men who have ruled over them for centuries, have reduced them to a level, whereby barely one sixth of the female population has had a minimum schooling of three years. Again, the Ulama insist on purdah; but they don't realise that almost ninety per cent of Muslim women cannot observe it because they go out into the fields to eke out a living for their families. Further, whatever the Islamic restrictions on the exercise of divorce, thousands of poor Muslim women are thrown out on the streets by men who misuse the Shariah. Though our

Prophet has enjoined upon men to protect the rights and interests of women, none of the rulers have ever bothered about it. General Zia-ul-Haq was once so moved in despair that he had announced that Pakistan could not progress unless women were taken out of, what he called, the *chador aur char diwari* (the veil and the four walls of home); but he failed to take any steps to ameliorate their condition. On the contrary, under pressure from the Ulama, he passed one measure after another, which was patently discriminatory against women.

Benazir has cited some instances; I can cite many more. The point to be considered, my Imams, is: whether men, as governors and rulers, have been just and fair to women? The verdict of history is totally against them. In case women are debarred from participating in public affairs, in case they are not allowed to stand equal to men — shoulder to shoulder — in every walk of life, they will continue to be degraded. They must not only be allowed, but prompted and trained to stand on their feet and to look after their own interest. Islam does not permit any kind of discrimination; it believes in equality of race and sex. Simone de Beauvoir, in her memorable work, *The Second Sex* has rightly asked how woman could show audacity, ardor, disinterestedness, grandeur when she was shut in a kitchen and her horizon restricted and her wings clipped.

You must have heard of the so-called Ansari Commission, appointed by General Zia-ul-Haq in Pakistan. Its recommendations are so atrocious that they must serve as a warning to all those, who are concerned about the future of Islam. If implemented, our women in desperation would turn away from their faith. The Commission recommended that women should be at least 50 years old before they could join politics and that too if husbands permited them; further that they could not travel without a male escort or join government or diplomatic service. Thank God, Zia himself rejected these recommendations; but it shows the mentality of persons, who claim to be guardians of Islam. No wonder, Syeda Abida Hussain, the sole female member of the Zia-appointed Majlis-e-Shura, asked Muslim women to prepare themselves to fight "the biggest *jihad* in Islam".

In the early period of Islam, when the Prophet was engaged in a life-and-death struggle, women openly and freely
helped the small band of believers. They did not participate
in the actual fighting on the battlefield but they carried food
for the combatants, nursed the injured, and took care of all
the needs of the fighting men. The Prophet's daughter,
Hadarat Fatimah was in the forefront; she tended the
wounded. His youngest wife , Hadarat Aisha used to tie
her gown upto her knees in order to carry water to the
warriors in the battle of Uhud. They moved freely among
men. They wore no veil. There are any number of traditions
to prove it. There is one tradition in the collection of Imam
Muslim which reports Umm Atiyyah as saying: "I took part
in seven battles with the Prophet of God, and I used to cook
food for the warriors, supply them with medicines and
dress up their wounds." It is also reported that Umm Salim
and other women of Medina administered medicines to the
wounded and supplied them drinking water. All these
traditions show that the Prophet did not want women to sit
at home but participate in outside activities. He permitted
them to pray in mosques along with men and render every
possible assistance both in war and administration. How
then could he say that a country ruled by a woman cannot
prosper? That tradition as quoted by Imam Bukhari has to
be understood in its historical perspective. It pertained to
Zorastrian , not Muslim rulers.

The Prophet's observation is said to have been made
when he was told that a daughter of the emperor of Persia,
Khusrow II had ascended the throne. He was slain by his
son Kavadh (Qobad II), who took over the reins. However,
after a few months Kavadh died. This was in 628. Then
there was utter anarchy for five years and one prince after
another was crowned as emperor. They did not rule for
more than a few months. Under this succession of short
term rulers, two daughters of Khusrow II — Purandukht
and Azarmidukht were crowned as empress one after another and overthrown by Yazadegerd III, a grandson
of Khusrow II, in 633. It is possible that the Prophet reacted
to this chaotic state of affairs and when informed of a
woman, who enjoyed no status in the Persia of those days,

having been crowned, opined that the act would bring no prosperity to the country. Again, we have to take into account the conditions prevailing at that time in Persia, which was a beehive of unbelief, corruption, nepotism and immorality; these cannot be compared with the present day conditions in Pakistan. It will, indeed, be a perversion of history to say that because Purandukth and Azarmidukth with their nefarious past and unholy linkage with some tribal chieftains, failed to bring prosperity to Persia, Bena-zir, a devout Muslim, a mature, educated and intelligent lady, who has been democratically elected by the faithful, will also fail to do so. Again, with all my respect to Imam Bukhari, it has generally been accepted that this particular tradition is rather weak because its original transmitter was a person who was flogged by Hadarat Umar for lying.

Imam Bukhari: But he had repented thereafter and was forgiven.

Ameer Ali: As you please, my venerable Imam. I further submit that it is not in consonance with the assessment by Allah of the rule of Bilqis, the Queen of Sheba; nor does it conform with the description by the Prophet of women as roses which can only spread fragrance.

The other Hadith or tradition by Tirmidhi also does not fit into the general attitude of the Prophet towards women; it puts women on a par with evil doers. It implies that under the rule of a woman death is preferable to life. It is inconcei-vable that a Prophet who held woman in such high esteem and gave her such an exalted position, could ever indulge in such a sweeping condemnation of them. I am unable to accept its authenticity.

Thus to attribute to our Prophet, who came as a mercy to all human kind, such traditions, which also seem totally torn out of context, is not fair. He was the greatest redeemer of oppressed women and indeed the strongest protector of their rights.

Coming to the question of woman moving freely in society, I admit my venerable Imams, that in modern times a ruler, whether male or female, is required to meet with those in authority, both at home and abroad; Islam, it is argued, does not allow such freedom to females. But then, every country has its culture; every faith, its style of functioning. There is no reason why a Muslim woman as a ruler would not adhere to her own code of conduct and yet be able to function as Head of State.

The great theologian, Ibn Hazm, in his well-known work, *Al-Muhalla* has said that a woman could "uncover her face and hands" while in public; so have many classical jurists. In fact, there is a consensus of the Ulama on this issue.

Besides, I don't agree with Rizvi that women should not be allowed seclusion or privacy with strange men; the history of the world shows that it is man who needs to be guarded from evil not the woman. The Prophet has repeatedly warned that "the evil is in man". Ever since Benazir has taken over the affairs of state in her hands, she has behaved in an exemplary manner. She is courteous but firm, competent without being over-bearing. She conducts herself with grace and dignity; she has done nothing to lower the prestige of Islam. She has been a devout Muslim, she prays five times a day, she fasts in the month of Ramadan and follows the religious code of conduct. Her first act on assuming office was to perform *Umra* — or pilgrimage to Mecca. She has also been a good mother; she spends all her spare time with her little son; her husband is happy with her. Her Government has waged a war against corruption; it has unearthed the crimes of heroin traffickers many of whom were close confidantes of the luminaries of the Zia regime. She has also stopped the illegal sales in international markets of arms and weapons given by America for the Afghan *mujahideen*. Strangely, these crimes against the state were committed by Zia's men under the umbrella of Islam. He introduced many so-called Islamic measures but they were used as cover by officials and politicians, to loot the people, impoverish the economy, and ruin the health of the youth. They posed as champions of Islam but they were worse than *manafiqun*. And they were all men. I ask, my Imams, what right have they to rule over us? Had it not been for Benazir, Pakistan would have been in a shambles; she has saved the country.

The test, therefore, of rulership should not be based on

the sex of the ruler but the character of the ruler, whether male or female.

And finally, may I have one last word since you have been so indulgent to me, my Honourable Imams; it has something to do with our approach to Islam, its traditions and its institutions in present times. I believe our Prophet wanted to give the best opportunities of growth and development to every Muslim, man or woman; not to imprison him or her in dogmas and rituals. He himself was a relentless rebel against all the cant and hypocrisy that prevailed in seventh century Arabia. As a Saudi Arabian scholar, Prof. Ziauddin Sardar of King Abdul Aziz University of Jeddah has observed: "By emphasizing the precision in the mechanics of prayer and ablution, length of beard and mode of dress, they (the Ulama) have lost sight of individual freedom, the dynamic nature of many Islamic injunctions, and the creativity and innovation that Islam fosters within its framework. They have founded intolerant, compulsive and tyrannical orders and have provided political legitimacy to despotic and nepotistic systems of government. They have closed and constricted many enquiring minds by their insistence on unobjective parallels, unending quibbles over semantics. They have divorced themselves from human needs and conditions. No wonder then that the majority of Muslims today pay little attention to them and even foster open hostility towards them".

I have finished, my most respectful Imams, and I entreat you in the name of that broad humanism, which is the hall-mark of our faith, to dismiss the petition and decree that a woman is as entitled in Islam to achieve the highest position in administration of a state as a man, provided she is faithful to the noble mission of our holy Prophet.

Brohi has relied on Freud; but many of his theories, as I pointed out, have been rejected. His pupil, Jung, had a better understanding of woman's position. He repeatedly reminded us that if woman remained in a state as she was, man could not progress very far. Hence according to him, the woman's problem has ceased to be her problem; it is more the man's problem. For if it is not solved satisfactorily, mankind would be held back; it could not advance.

I thank you, my most venerable Imams, for the patient hearing that all of you have given me and the grace and dignity with which you have conducted these proceedings. I also thank my learned friend for bearing with me; it was, indeed, gracious of him.

Imam Ghazali: I hope both sides have had their full say and have made the presentation they wished to make.

Brohi: Yes, my reverend Imams, I am most grateful.

Ameer Ali: My Imams, we have, indeed, had the most fair and patient hearing.

Imam Ghazali: Very well, then. The case of the petitioners against Benazir Bhutto now stands closed. There will be no more evidence or argument. The Council will pronounce its judgement tomorrow.

11

The Final Judgement

Ninth Day

Much before the arrival of the members of the Supreme Shariah Council, the hall of Al-Ahzar was filled to capacity; a huge crowd waited outside. Everyone was anxious to hear the verdict which would decide the fate of the powerful Muslim state. There was hardly any indication about the outcome. Benazir was seated with her father, Zulfiqar Ali Bhutto on one side and her husband Asif Zardari on the other. Her mother Nusrat was on the right of Bhutto. President Hosni Mubarak was present along with many of his cabinet colleagues; so was the Shaikhul Azhar and the other religious dignitaries. It was indeed, a historic moment, unparalleled in the annals of Islam.

Imam Ghazali spoke as soon as the Imams took their seats: "My brothers and sisters in Islam. I begin in the name of Allah, the Beneficient and the Merciful. For eight days we have heard the arguments in this matter from both sides and have benefitted greatly. Of course, my most learned colleagues embody in themselves all the depth of learning. They needed no enlightenment. They are the most respected among Muslims because of their piety, wisdom and spiritual attainments. Much of what I know I have learnt from them; they are, indeed, our beacon light.

"I have had a chequered life. From my early youth I have, sometimes recklessly, launched into the search for the truth, acquainting myself with different theological systems, varying philosophies and a host of commentaries and traditions. I have tried to probe into every dark recess. I have made an assault on every problem. I have plunged into every abyss. I have scrutinised every doctrine. All this I

have done so that God might help me to distinguish the
true from the false, the real from the unreal. If I met a
philosopher, I tried to get at the root of his philosophy. If I
met a theologian, I tried to understand the essence of his
scholasticism; if I met a Ṣufi, I tried to fathom the secret of
his mysticism. To thirst after a comprehension of things as
they really were, was my habit; it became, in course of time,
my second nature. Consequently,I could never accept *taqlid*
or imitation; I questioned inherited beliefs and worked to
bring about harmony and order out of the theological chaos
that prevailed. I, therefore, came to be known as a reconciler; that is why my learned colleagues chose me, though I
am very much their junior, to head this Council. I have no
words to thank them; their confidence in me is God's blessing In this case I have done my best to reconcile their
conflicting views; I am sorry to say that I have not fully
succeeded."

This was a forewarning that the verdict might not be
unanimous.

Imam Ghazali proceeded: " For my part,I have been
influenced by one undisputed fact, that there is no specific
bar in the Quran against a woman being a ruler. Nor is it
mentioned in any one of the treatises on Government written by the classical jurists from Farabi to Ibn Khaldun.
Mawardi refers to many disqualifications but this one does
not figure in them. What I tried to find out was whether
Benazir, irrespective of her sex, qualified to be Prime Minister of Pakistan. Now, under the Constitution of Pakistan she
is not the Head of the State. The President, Gulam Ishaq
Khan is the Head and he has been entrusted with several
executive functions. He is not just nominal. He appoints
the Prime Minister and he can dismiss him or her. Likewise, he appoints the three defence chiefs and presides
over the Defence Council. He has also the power to dissolve
the National Assembly. True, the Prime Minister also enjoys a great deal of executive authority but he or she is
subordinate to the President; in short, power is shared
between them. Hence she is not the exclusive or supreme
leader.

"Again, President Ishaq Khan has spoken favourably of

Benazir. He has said that she is 'educated, cultured and talented' and further that she is 'endowed with the best qualities of leadership and the foresight of a statesman'. I cannot ignore this assessment. Also, the National Assembly has given its allegiance to her. Her advent has helped in repairing the schism. She has brought some sort of order and peace in the troubled areas. I have always held that order has to be preferred to chaos. I, therefore, hold that it is in the larger interest of the Muslims of Pakistan that Benazir Bhutto should continue as Prime Minister.

"I have deliberately not touched on the religious controversies because I feel that my learned colleagues, from whom I have learnt the religious fundamentals as well as the directive principles are better qualified to dilate upon them; but I share the sentiments expressed by my pupil Ibn Tumart about women; earlier I must confess I had erred in this respect. In one of my books *Nasihatul Muluk*, or Counsel to Rulers I myself had listed no less than 18 points against women; those were the common perceptions at that time. Since then the world has changed much and the Quran enjoins upon us to change in accordance with the times. I was one of the first to take note of changes in my times and reconcile the prevalent demands with the fundamentals of our faith and I thank God for the service I was able to render to Islam. Now once again, a change in our old and outmoded approach has become inevitable. I repeat that there is no warrant either in the Quran or the Hadith for us to hold that a woman cannot rise to the highest position; if Rabia, the Sufi Saint, could reach the sublime heights spiritually, there should be no bar on Benazir to be Prime Minister of Pakistan."

Imam Abu Hanifa, the greatest of the Imams, spoke in his soft, sedate manner; after reciting a few Quranic verses and offering his salutations he declared that his "approach to religion had always been broad-based. The more I pray to Allah the more I am convinced that our actions should be guided by reason. I believe that faith has to be strengthened by reason. Our beloved Prophet has said, 'God has not created anything better than reason, or anything more perfect or more beautiful than reason.' Allah has admonished

the faithful in the Quran: 'Think deeply O ye, who understand.'

"I was accused that I laid too much emphasis on analogy.
I admit I consider analogy as a valuable aid to meet new
challenges; but I never gave it undue importance. Imam
Baqir on his second visit to Mecca, asked me whether I
contradicted the traditions of his grandfather, the Prophet,
on the basis of analogy. I told him most respectfully: 'God
forbid, my Imam. Who can contradict the Hadith?'

He said, 'I understand you do.'

I said, 'May I be permitted to ask you a question?'

He said, 'Yes'.

I asked, 'Who is the weaker one, man or woman?'

Imam Baqir replied, 'Woman'.

I then enquired, 'Which of them should get a larger share
in inheritance?'

Imam Baqir was puzzled but said, 'Man'.

I explained, 'Now, if I had been making deductions by
analogy, I should have said that woman should get the
larger share because she deserved it more. But I did not'.

"Imam Baqir was so satisfied with my reply that he blessed me. I laid the greatest emphasis on the Quran and the
Hadith; but where I was convinced that a Hadith was a
concoction, and most Hadith were, then I resorted to reason and deduced conclusions on the basis of analogy.

"In this case I prefer to take the totality of our Prophet's
approach to women, than go by a Hadith here or there. The
Quran also gives ample evidence of the equality of the two
sexes. The husband has an edge over the wife in family
affairs but from this we cannot conclude that a man is
superior to a woman in every respect. There is no basis for
this either in the Quran or the Sunnah.

"Islam cuts across all barriers, including that of the high
and the low; it treats every believer as equal. That is why it
triumphed in diverse countries and among diverse races
from one end of the earth to the other. It was able to
accommodate the faithful everywhere and absorb within its
world people of different habits and customs. By its very
nature Islam is all-absorbing; it cannot be restrictive. It is
broadbased, liberal and tolerant. The Quran has proclai-

med Islam as the religion of humanity; it has described our Prophet as mercy to all mankind. My effort has been to make the Shariah as liberal as possible. Hence it is not possible for me to deny Benazir the right of rulership. She is as entitled to the high office as any male Muslim.

"My view may not be liked by some Ulama here. During my time I faced a worse situation. Most Ulama ostracised me; but I was not worried. I never cared for popularity; nor did I hanker after office.

"The Umaiyyad governor of Kufa offered me the post of a Qadi or judge. I refused. He was annoyed and he jailed me. I suffered but did not relent. Likewise, the Abbasid Caliph insisted that I should accept the office of Chief Justice; I declined. He put me in prison. Why have I then associated myself with this Council? The answer is simple. Here the issue is not of an individual but of the community. Will Muslims of Pakistan be ill-served, if Benazir, a woman, continues to head their government? In my humble opinion the answer is, no; in case she fails to serve Islam and her people properly then the answer will be, yes but that would be, applicable as much to a male ruler as to a female ruler."

Imam Malik then spoke in a firm voice: "May Allah be praised and peace be upon our beloved Prophet. My salutations to all of you. I agree with Imam Ghazali and Imam Abu Hanifa. In the Quran there is no specific injunction, which can prevent a woman from participation in public affairs; nor is there anything in the Sunnah. In fact the living traditions of Medina point in favour of her participating in politics. For instance, during the Prophet's lifetime, his youngest wife Hadrat Aisha took part in discussions pertaining to the affairs of state; later during the caliphate of Hadrat Ali, she led the troops against the Caliph in the battle of the camel. Similarly, Hadrat Fatimah, the daughter of our holy Prophet, was actively involved in the campaign for making her husband the Caliph; her house was the centre of activities with the result that Hadrat Umar warned her: 'We love you the most as the daughter of our beloved Prophet but if you do not cease your conspiracy against us, I shall burn down your house.' Again Asma, the daughter of Hadrat Abu Bakr, stood undaunted by the side of her son Abdulla bin al-Zubair in the war against al-Hajjaj, the dreaded Umayyad Viceroy. There is also the well-known case of the wife of Habib bin Maslama, when he was proceeding on one of the expeditions in the cause of Islam. 'Where are you going?' she asked. He replied, 'Either to the enemy's camp or Paradise.' 'I shall be there before you,' she said and reached with her troops at the enemy's camp before her husband. Also, Hadrat Umar had appointed a woman to one of the key posts in his administration — Shifa' bint Abdallah controlled the markets in Medina.

Imam Malik continued: "I came across thousands of traditions, but none, which said that woman could not be a ruler. There are, no doubt, women and women; most are dependent on men; many are *naqisal aql wadin*, lacking in wisdom and faith, but there are also notable exceptions and our religion recognises their worth. In deciding a case I always took into account *al-Masalih al-Mursalah* or what is called public interest. If there is no specific verse in the Quran or any specific instance in the Sunnah, then the test should be what is in the public interest. In this case, neither side has produced any specific Quranic verses or specific Hadith, which favour or debar a woman from being a ruler; what has been urged before us is by implication. A better course will be to apply the test of public interest. Benazir has been chosen by the elected representatives of the people as their leader; she assumed office under abnormal circumstances. Since neither the Quran nor any Hadith specifically disqualfies her, why should we disturb the people's choice?"

The congregation was keenly waiting for Imam Shafi'1 to speak for even Imam Ghazali accepted him as master and Muslims in general have hailed him as a restorer of the faith. He began by praising Allah and the last Prophet and said that the opinion of any theologian, however learned, could not supercede a Hadith, which was binding on Muslims. "In this case, your attention has been drawn to two Hadith; one by my colleague on the Council, Imam Bukhari and the other by Imam Tirmidhi.I accept their authenticity; the two Imams command our highest respect. But I would like to judge the relevance of these Hadith in their proper context; they cannot be taken as general condemnation of women, even if the latter were called upon to rule. Such a deduction does not conform with the Prophet's outlook or the various measures he took to uplift women; nor is it consistent with the favourable references to Bilqis, the Queen of Sheba, in the Quran (27 : 24-46).

"Islam never accepted the Christian concept that woman was evil; she is as much *ashraful makhluqat* or'the noblest of creation' as men. There are any number of references to her nobility in the Quran and the Hadith. I am emboldened to assert this on the basis of the Prophet's over-all conduct. There is a Hadith which attributes to him the words: 'poetry is the flute of the devil'. I don't challenge its accuracy; but it has to be understood in its proper context, which some-times has to be deducted from his outlook. Will we be justified in holding that the Prophet considered all poetry to be evil? If so, does it fit into his general attitude to poets? No. He is reported to have been most appreciative of poets. He used to listen to the poetry of Hassan bin Thabit, Kaab bin Malik, Abdullah bin Rawahah and several other Arab poets of his time and praised their compositions. He also enjoyed the poems of al-Khansa, the most celebrated Arab poetess. Obviously, the reference to poetry being 'the flute of the devil' applied to vicious poetry; likewise the re-ference in the two Hadith, to the rule by women, must be construed to apply to immoral and corrupt women, as symbolised by the two daughters of Khusro and not to all women.

"There is another aspect to this issue, which cannot be ignored. Yes, a wife is subordinate to a husband; but I am unable to hold that woman, in general, is subordinate to man. The distinction may be subtle but it has to be clearly understood. Man is not the totality of existence as God is. God is neither man nor woman. He encompasses everyone and everything. Woman is an entity by herself; she is not a part of man. The Prophet is reported to have said that he was appreciative of or esteemed three things: perfume, prayers, and women. Like perfume and prayers women bring fragrance and fulfilment in man's life.

"I am not much enamoured of my faculty of reasoning; in fact the more experience I gain of the problems of this world, the more convinced I become of my own helplessness. Nay, the more knowledge I acquire the more aware I become of the extent of my ignorance. I treasure the Quran, the Hadith and the Sunnah more than my reasoning but I seek guidance through them by the application of my reason, with which God has endowed me. My faith, therefore, is unbounded; my reasoning, limited.

"After the Quran, the Hadith and the Sunnah, I give the greatest importance to *ijma* or the consensus of the learned; this consensus, in a way, represents the conscience of the 'collectivity'. And also its will. As the Prophet has said, 'the collectivity never errs'; in this case the learned are divided but the majority in the "collectivity" has expressed its confidence in the leadership of Benazir. She has, therefore, received the backing of the community and the community never errs. In the National Assembly she received the allegiance of 148 representatives against 55 — an overwhelming number and among her 55 opponents there were a number of activist women. Does this not show that opposition to her is not religious but political? I may also mention that I learnt a great deal of the Sunna sitting at the feet of the great lady Nafisah, a descendant of Hadrat Ali, in this very city, then known as Fustat. After giving careful thought I am, therefore, inclined to agree with the previous Imams."

Imam Hanbal, first recited *surah fatiha* in his rich, melodious voice, and then said that any kind of innovation was destructive of Islam. He urged that the Quranic injunctions had to be strictly followed. He elaborated it thus: "On the issue before the Council I have no doubt in my mind that it is not a woman's function to rule; it is man's. I firmly believe that the whole social fabric would be disrupted if man started doing woman's work and woman man's. It will disturb the process of procreation, with the result that children will suffer grievously and family life will be destroyed. Why do we think a family is less important than a state? Family, in fact, is the basis of human progress. The Quran has laid the greatest stress on it. Our beloved Prophet has said, 'The best of you is he who is best to his family'.

"The Quran has indicated that man is a degree higher than woman; not only as between a husband and a wife but also between a son and a daughter or between a father and a mother. All females inherit half the share in inheritance as compared to the males. Of course, there is no specific injunction in the Quran that a woman cannot be a ruler but its general trend is unmistakable. I may be orthodox and rigid in my approach but I believe this is the only way to protect the purity of the faith and to rescue it from the innovations and distortions that have crept into it. I don't go by my instinct, but by what is in the Quran or the Sunnah.

"Once a learned man from Khurasan came to me and presented a compendium of my views. I threw it away. He was much upset as he had worked hard on it. I told him I was fallible; only the Quran and the Sunnah are infallible. Likewise the Abbasid Caliph, Mustasim wanted me to give up my rigidity; he asked me to be pragmatic. I refused. He got me publicly flogged and put me in prison. But it did not break my resolve; it did not change my conviction.

"I don't believe in compromise; I go by the Quran and the Hadith. An enquiring mind is the devil's workshop. Allah has warned us: 'Some people before you did ask questions and on that account lost their faith' (3 : 104:5). We must hold fast to our faith. Hence I most respectfully disagree with the views of my learned colleagues. I am convinced that Benazir Bhutto should go back to her home, look after her husband and take care of her child; therein alone lies her salvation.

"I had been party to an earlier judgement, delivered by our President, Imam Ghazali, holding that Islam considers man and woman equal. I don't retract from it. But it does not mean that there is no division of functions between the two. A teacher cannot do the work of a doctor; or a salesman that of a nurse. The division between man and woman is natural. It is ordained by God. Where is the need for upsetting it? The more we question, the more confused we will become."

Imam Bukhari, whose *Al-Jami Al Sahih* or book of traditions is considered the most sacred after the Quran, said after invoking the usual salutations that he would not indulge in any hair-splitting. "I have also carefully listened to the arguments advanced by both sides. Despite the fact that the Hadith; recorded by me, has been under attack, I have kept an open mind. That is expected of a judge. Our second Caliph, Hadrat Umar wrote to Abu Musa on his appointment as Qadi as follows:

'Try to understand the depositions that are made before you because it will be useless to consider a plea that is not valid. Consider all equal before you in the court and (consider them equal) in giving your attention to them so that the highly placed may not expect you to be partial and the humble may not despair of justice from you. The claimant must produce evidence. An oath must be taken. It is permissible to have compromise among Muslims but not an agreement through which *haram* (unlawful) would be turned into *halal* (lawful) and vice versa. If you have given a judgement yesterday and today you may arrive to a correct opinion upon re-thinking, you must not feel prevented from retracting from your first judgement, because justice is primeval, and it is better to retreat than to continue in error.'

Imam Bukhari continued: "I would have retracted from the position I had taken had I been convinced to the contrary; but I have not been. I try to go to the root of a matter and to arrive at the truth. I have been, in fact, merciless in rejecting the spurious and the false sayings of the Prophet. I examined more than 600,000 Hadith and accepted only 7,397. The tests I applied were the strictest. I am, therefore, not prepared to concede that the Hadith in question is not reliable; it is in conformity with several Quranic verses and the Sunnah of the Prophet and the approach of his Companions. I am of the opinion that Pakistan cannot prosper under a woman".

Finally, the second most important compiler of Hadith, Imam Muslim, spoke; he praised Allah and his beloved Prophet and said that he was confused after listening to the differing views of the most pious and learned Imams. He clarified; "In fact I am in two minds. On the one side is the Hadith, as recorded by my own teacher, Imam Bukhari which prohibits a women from being a ruler; and on the other side, the arguments of Imam Abu Hanifa and Imam Shafi'i. I have also my differences with my teacher as far as the recording of Hadith is concerned; to me the difference between *Haddathana* (he narrated to us) and *Akhbarana* (he informed us) is important. This particular Hadith is in the second category and therefore not as sound. But I cannot reject it as untrue; I have an element of doubt, which may be justified or not. Of course there are many Hadith recorded by me which Imam Bukhari has regarded as untrustworthy; someone has counted them and the number is as high as 625. Hence there are differences between us, though I respect him as my leader. In regard to this particular Hadith or the one recorded by Tirmidhi, I did not come across either of them. Nor any other narration to the effect that a woman could not be a ruler. Also, I must admit I did not find any Hadith, which said she could rule either. I would, therefore, not like to express any opinion on this issue."

After all the Imams had spoken, the President, Imam Ghazali, summed up their findings. "The matter before us is, indeed, complex; we have deliberated on all aspects of a woman's status and position in Islam. For long hours, arguments and counter-arguments went on. I don't think there was any point which was not thrashed out. At one stage I wanted to follow what Imam Shafi'i had once done, when he was asked a question. He did not reply. On being questioned 'Why dost thou not answer? he said 'Because I am not sure which is better, my silence or my reply'. I found myself in the same dilemma. However, we realise the gravity of the situation and we have carefully weighed the pros and cons of the matter. Each one of us has spoken and given his opinion. On the basis of these I now declare that the verdict of the Council, by a majority of four against two, with one abstention, is that Benazir Bhutto can continue as Prime Minister of Pakistan."

"This is no verdict; this not even *ijma* or consensus of the learned; it is also not backed by the consensus of the community. Everything is by majority and there is no place for majority in Islam", cried Maulana Ihteshamul Haq, one of the petitioners.

'That is not correct. There is bound to be *ikhtilaf* (differences of opinion) among the learned. Our Prophet had said that 'difference of opinion among Muslims is a bounty of Allah', remarked Imam Abu Hanifa.

Imam Malik added, "*Ijma* (consensus) does not mean unanimity; it means the opinion of the generality. Islam is a practical religion; it encourages *ijtihad* or independent thinking as an aid to finding a solution. *Ijithad* is bound to result in difference of opinion and hence *ijma* can at best be the consensus of the largest number and not necessarily of all".

Mohammad Abdul, one of the greatest rectors of Al-Azhar, rose from his seat and pointed out that *ijma* by majority had the sanction of such eminent theologians as Tabari, Abu Bakr Razi and Shah Waliuallah. Imam Abu Hanifa asked the petitioner whether his reaction to the verdict would have been the same, had it gone in his favour.

"It would have been binding on the believers then", said Maududi, "because it would have had the support of Hadith".

Ibn Taimiyya interjected, "May I also add, Sirs, that as the Sunnah cannot abrogate the Quran, *ijma* also cannot abrogate the Hadith".

"True," said Imam Shafi;i "but we have to be sure first that it is absolutely authentic; secondly, that it covers this particular situation and thirdly that there are other Hadith, to back it."

"Dependence on books of traditions is not always reliable," explained Imam Ghazali. "In fact their compilation was an innovation. No book of traditions existed during the time of the Companions of our Prophet who discouraged such compilation. Hadith began to be compiled 125 years after the passing away of our Prophet".

At this stage, Ibn Qutayba, one of the greatest upholders of Hadith, who had acted as a judge under the Abbasid Caliph al-Mutawakkil, stood up and requested to be heard.

"It will be our pleasure to hear you", said Imam Ghazali.

"The truth," Ibn Qutayba submitted, "is more likely to be

contained in *ijma* than in Hadith, which is subject to many vicissitudes, such as negligence of those who handed it down, confused explanations, the abrogation which may have occurred, the unreliability of informants, the existence of contradictory Hadith ... The *ijma* of the community is free from such vicissitudes."

"Is it true that the Ulama were not able to convince the framers of the Constitution of Pakistan that the Head of the State had to be a Muslim male?" enquired Imam Malik.

"The framers were all political Muslims," replied Maududi. "They were not qualified to question us."

"You are going back to your old argument", commented Imam Abu Hanifa.

"Is it not a fact that even Zia-ul-Haq, who is known to be your disciple, did not incorporate such a provision in his constitutional framework?" enquired Imam Shafi'i.

"It was a blunder on his part," admitted Maududi. "And that is why we are in this mess".

The Imams started to look at one another with a feeling of unease when suddenly Ihteshamul Haq bellowed: "How is it possible, my venerable Imams, for persons in our position to accept a woman like Benazir Bhutto as our ruler?"

Imam Ghazali declared firmly: "We cannot go back to where we began; we cannot allow the matter to be reopened", and adjourned the Council *sine die*.

ACKNOWLEDGEMENTS

I consulted many books in English, Urdu, Arabic and Persian while writing *The Trial of Benazir* but I must acknowledge the debt that I owe to the authors, editors, translators and publishers of the following in particular. From many of their works, I have taken extracts and used them at appropriate places:

A

Ali, Abdullah Yusuf: *The Holy Quran.* Beirut, 1968.

Mauudi, Syed Abul a'la: *The Meaning of the Quran.* (translated into the English). 4 vols. Delhi, 1970.

Azad Abul Kalam: *Tarjuman al-Quran.* (English translation by Syed Abdul Latif). 3 vols. 1 & 2, Bombay 1967. Vol. 3, Hyderabad, 1978.

Bukhari Imam: *Sahih al-Bukhari.* (translated into the English by Muhammad Ali.). 9 vols. Madina, 1974.

Muslim, Imam: *Sahih Muslim.* (rendered into the English by Abdul Hamid Siddiqi. 4 vols. Lahore, 1973.

Malik, Imam: *Muatta.* (translated into the English with exhaustive notes by Muhammad Rahimuddin.). New Delhi, 1981.

Al-Baghawi, Abu Muhammad al-Husain: *Mishkat al-Masabih.* (translated into the English by James Robson). Vols. I - IV. Lahore, 1973.

Ayoub, Mahmud: *Quran and its interpreters.* Vol. I New York, 1984.

T.P. Hughes: *A Dictionary of Islam.* Delhi, 1973.

Mahmud, Qasim (ed.): *Islami Encylopaedia:* Karachi, 1984.

Glasse, Cyril: *The Concise Encyclopaedia of Islam.* London, 1989.

Muhammad Ali: *A Manual of Hadith: Lahore,* n.d.
     The Religion of Islam: Lahore, 1950.

V.K.: *Women, Status of.* in *Encyclopaedia Britannica.* Marcopaedia, Vol. 19, Chicago, 1974.

Gibb, H.A.R. & J.H. Kramers (ed.): *Shorter Encylopaedia of Islam.* New York, 1965.

B

Ahmad, Ilyas: *The Social Contract and Islamic State.* New Delhi, 1982.
Ahmad, Khurshid (ed.): *Islam: Its Meaning and Message.* London, 1975:
Arberry, A.J.: *Religion in the Middle East:* Vol. 2. Cambridge, 1969.
Ahmad, Sayed Riyaz: *Maulana Maududi and the Islamic State.* Lahore, 1976.
Ahmed, Aziz: *Islamic Modernization in India and Pakistan.* London, 1967.
Ameer Ali, Syed: *The Spirit of Islam.* Delhi, 1968.
  A short History of the Saracens. Delhi, 1981.
Aslam Muhammad: *Muslim Conduct of State.* Lahore, 1974.
Askari, Hasan: *Society and State in Islam - an Introduction.* Delhi, 1978.
Arari, Farah (ed.): *Women of Iran.* London, 1983.
Ansari, Mohammad Anis and Masood, Arshad (ed.): *Aligarh Law Journal: Mahmood Number:* Vol. V. Aligarh, 1973.
Ahmed, Ishtiaq: *The concept of an Islamic State.* London, 1987.
Anjum, Khaliq (ed.): *Sayyid Sulaiman Nadvi.* (Urdu text). New Delhi, 86.
Baijon, D.D. Jr.: *The Reform and Religious Ideas of Sir Sayed Ahmad Khan.* Lahore, 1958.
Baveja, Malik Ram: *Woman in Islam.* Hyderabad, n.d.
Bernard, Lewis: *The Emergence of Modern Turkery.* Oxford, 1968.
Bhutto, Benazir: *Daughter of the East.* London, 1988.
Bloom, Allan: *The Closing of the American Mind.* New York, 1988.
Binder, Leonard: *Religion and Politics in Pakistan.* Berkeley, 1963.
Brijbhushan, Jamila: *Muslim Women — In Purdah and out of it.* New Delhi, 1980.
Burki, Shahid Javed: *Pakistan Under Bhutto: 1971-1977.* London, 1980.
Coulson, N.J.: *A History of Islamic Law.* Endinburgh, 1971.
Crone, Patricia and Hinds, Martin: *God's Caliph: Religious Authority in the First Centuries of Islam.* London, 1986.
Cragg, Kenneth: *The Call of the Minaret.* Oxford, 1956.
Cudsi, Alexander S. and Alie Dessouki E.H.: *Islam and Power.* London, 1981.
De Beauvoir, Simone: *The Second Sex.* New York, 1974.
Dekmejian, R. Hrair. : *Islam in Revolution.* New York, 1985.
Dessouki, Ali E. Hilal.: *Islamic Resurgence in the Arab World.* New York, 1982.
Dodge, B. Al-Ashar: *Religious and Political Trends in Modern Egypt.* Washington, 1950.
Doi, I. Abdur Rahman: *Shariah: The Islamic Law.* London, 1984.
Donohne, John, J and Esposito, John (ed.): *Islam in Transition.* Oxford, 1982.
Doyle, Phyllis: *A History of Political Thought.* London, 1963.
Greer, Germaine: *The Femal Ennuch.* London, 1971.

Edib, Halide: *Conflict of East and West in Turkey.* Lahore, 1935.
Enayat, Hamid: *Modern Islamic Political Thought.* Austin, 1982.
Esposito, John, L.(ed): *Voices of Resurgent Islam.* New York, 1984.
                              Islam and Politics. New York, 1984.
Falahi, Javid Ahsan: *Aurat Islam Ki Nazar Mein.* (translated in the Urdu from the Arabic work by Albahi Alkholi). Delhi, n.d.
Fallaci, Oriana: *Interview with History.* Boston, 1976.
Farrukh, Omar A: *Ibn Taimiyya on Public and Private Law in Islam.* Beirut, 1966.
Fayzee, Asaf A.A.: *Modern Approach to Islam.* Bombay, 1963.
                        Outlines of Muhammadan Law. London, 1964.
Ferna, Elizabeth Warnock and Bezizgan, Basima Qattan: *Middle Eastern Muslim Women Speak.* Austin, 1980.
Frya, R.N.(ed.): *Islam and the West.* The Hague, 1957.
Ghazali, Imam: *The Book of Knowledge.* (translated into the English by Nabih Amin Faris). Beirut, 1962.
               Ihya Ulum-Id-Din (translated from the Arabic into the English by Fazul-ul-Karim): Book I to IV: Kitab Bhavan, New Delhi, 1982.
               Mukashafitul Qulub (translated from the Arabic into the Urdu by Taqaaddus Ali Khan): Ghaziabad, 1976.
Gibb H.A.R.: *Modern Trends in Islam.* Chicago, 1947.
Goldziher, Ignaz: *Introduction to Islamic Theology and Law.* Princeton, 1981.
Gray Seymouir: *Beyond The Veil.* New York, 1983.
Gokap, Zya: *Turkish Nationalism and Western Civilization:* (ed. and translated by Niyazi Berkes). New York, 1959.
Grunebaum G.E. Von: *Modern Islam: The Search for Cultural Identity.* Berkeley, 1962.
Goldziher, Ignaz: *Muslim Studies:* Vol. Two. London, 1971.
Beck, Lois and Keddie, Nikki (ed): *Women in the Muslim World.* Cambridge, 1982.
Haddad, Yvonne Yazbeck: *Contemporary Islam and the Challenge of History.* Albany, 1982.
Haykal, Muhammad Husayn: *The Life of Muhammad.* (translated into the English by Ismail Ragi A. Faruji). New York, 1976.
Hyman Anthony and others: *Pakistan; Zia and After.* London, 1988.
Hakim, Khalifa Abdul: *Islamic Ideology.* Lahore, 1951.
Hamidullah M.: *The Muslim Conduct of State.* Lahore, 1945.
Hasan, Farooq: *The Concept of State and Law in Islam.* London, 1979.
Hawwa, Saeed: *The Muslim Brotherhood.* Delhi, 1983.
Hitti, Phillip K: *History of the Arabs.* London 1974.
                    Makers of Arab History. New York, 1971.
Hussaini, Ishak Musa: *The Moslem Brethren.* Beirut, 1956.
Ibn Khaldun: *The Muqaddimah: An Introduction to History.* (translated from Arabic by Franz Rosental). 3 Vols. New York, 1958.
Imran, Muhammed: *Ideal Woman in Islam.* Delhi, 1986.
Iqbal, Afzal: *Islamisation of Pakistan.* Delhi, 1984.
Iqbal Javid: *Ideology of Pakistan.* Lahore, 1971.

Ishaq, Muhammad: *Sirat Rasul Allah.* (translated with Introduction & Notes by A. Guillaume). Oxford, 1955.

Iqbal, Mohammed: *The Reconstruction of Religious Thought In Islam.* Lahore, 1971.

Javid Nama. (translated from the Persian with introduction and Notes by A.J. Arberry). London, 1966.

Islahi, Muhammad Yusuf: *Zikra Digest:* Rampur: February & March, 1989.

Jansen, G.H: *Militant Islam.* London, 1979.

Jalbani, S.N.: *Teachings of Shah Waliyullah.* Lahore, 1967.

James O. Piscatori: *Islam in a World of Nation States.* Cambridge, 1986.

Keddie, N.R.: *An Islamic Response to Imperialism.* Los Angeles, 1968.

Religion and Politics in Iran. London, 1983.

Kedourie, E.: *The Middle East and the West.* London, 1964.

Afghani and Abduh. London, 1966.

Islam in the Modern World. New York, 1980.

Kepel, Gilles: *The Prophet and Pharaoh.* London, 1985.

Khan, Qamaruddin: *The Political Though of Ibn Taymiyah.* Delhi, 1988.

Khaldun, S. Al-Hasry: *Three Reformers.* Beirut, 1966.

Lacey, Robert: *The Kingdom — Arabia and The House of Saud.* New York, 1981.

Latif, Syed Abdul: *Bases of Islamic Culture.* Hyderabad, 1959,

Levy, Reuben: *The Social Structure of Islam.* Cambridge, 1971.

Lemu, Aisha B. and Heeren, Fatima: *Woman in Islam.* Aligarh, 1977.

Lings, Martin: *Islam and the Future.* Kuwait, 1987.

Macdonald, Duncan B.: *Development of Muslim Theology.*

Mahmood, Tahir: *Personal Law in Islamic Countries.* New Delhi, 1987.

Malcolm, Sir John: *Tarikhe Iran Vol. 1* (Persian manuscript).

Maududi, Syed Abul a'la: *The Islamic Law and Constitution.* Bombay, 1986.

Fundamentals of Islam. Bombay, 1978.

Purdah and the Status of Woman. Delhi, 1974.

Khilafat-o-Mulukiat (Urdu text). Delhi, 1983.

Mill, John Stuart: *The Subjection of Women.* London, 1966.

Mottaheden, Roy: *The Mantle of the Prophet.* London, 1986.

Munir, Muhammed: *From Jinnah to Zia.* Lahore, 1979. London, 1986.

Millets, Kate: *Sexual Politics.* New York, 1978.

Nadvi, Abul Hasan Ali: *Saviours of Islamic Spirit.* Lucknow 1955.

Noamani, Shibli: *Al Faruq.* (Urdu text). Delhi, n.d.

Sirat-T-Numan. (Urdu text). Vol. I and II. Azamgazh. n.d.

Nasr, Seyyed Hossein: *Traditional Islam in the Modern World.* London, 1987.

Nadvi, Saiyid Sulaiman: *Siratun Nabi.* (Urdu text). Vol. III (1958); Vol. IV (1974); Vol. V (1962), Azamgrah.

Pickthall, M: *Cultural Side of Islam.* Lahore, 1961.

Pearl, David: *A textbook on Muslim Law.* London, 1979.

Qadri, Anwar: *Islamic Jurisprudence in the Modern World.* Lahore, 1981.
Qutb, Sayyid: *In the Shade of the Quran:* Vol: 30. London, 1979.
        This Religion of Islam. Beirut n.d.
Qutb, Muhammad: Islam — *The Misunderstood Religion.* Delhi, 1968.
Rahman, Fazlur: *Islam and Modernity.* London, 1982.
        Islam. London, 1966.
Robert, Roberts: *The Social Laws of the Quran.* London, 1971.
Rodinson, Maxime: *Muhammad.* (translated into the English by Anne
Carter). London, 1971.
Rotman, Sheila M.: *Woman's Proper Place.* New York, 1978.
Rothschild, Jon: *Forbidden Agendas.* London, 1976.
Rosenthal, E.I.J.: *Islam in the Modern National State.* Cambridge, 1965.
Salem Azzam (ed.): *Islam and Contemporary Society.* London, 1982.
Schacht, Joseph: *The Origins of Muhammadan Jurisprudence.* Oxford,
1975.
Shabbir, Mohammad: *The Authority and Authenticity of Hadith.* New
Delhi, 1982.
Siddiqi, Muhammad Iqbal: *Islam Forbids Free Mixing of Men and Wo-*
men. Delhi, 1988.
Siddiqi, Muhammad Saeed: *The Blessed Women of Islam.* Delhi, 1983.
Sivan, Emmanuel: *Radical Islam.* London, 1985.
Smith, W.C.: *Islam in Modern History.* Princeton, 1960.
Sherwani, Haroon Khan: *Studies in Muslim Political Thought and Admi-*
nistration. Lahore, 1942.
Siddiqi, M. Mazheruddin: *Women in Islam.* Lahore, 1479.
Sadat, Jehan: *A Woman of Eqypt.* London, 1987.
Umm-i-Faruq: *Khawateen, Rasul-i-Akram ki Nazar mein.* (Urdu text).
New Delhi, 1988.
Watt, Montgomery W.: *The Faith and Practice of Al-Ghazali.* Lahore,
1963.
                The Formative Period of Islamic Thought. Edin-
burgh, 1973.

                Muhammad at Mecca, Oxford, '1953.
                Muhammad at Medina, Oxford, 1956.
                Islamic Political Thought. Endinburgh, 1968.
Wajdi, Fareed: *Al-Muratul Muslimah.* (translated from Arabic into the
Urdu by Abul Kalam Azad). New Delhi, 1987.
Wahid, Syed Abdul: *Thoughts and Reflections of Iqbal.* Lahore, 1964.
Weiss, Anita M.: *Islamic Reassertion in Pakistan.* New York, 1986.
Young, Ian: *The Private Life of Islam.* London, 1974.
Zakaria, Rafiq: *The Struggle Within Islam.* New Delhi, 1989.
Ziauddin, Sardar: *The Future of Muslim Civilisation.* London 1979.